D0465697

BEST OF

Venice

Damien Simonis

How to use this book

Colour-Coding & Maps

Each chapter has a colour code along the banner at the top of the page which is also used for text and symbols on maps (eg all venues reviewed in the Highlights chapter are orange on the maps). The fold-out maps inside the front and back covers are numbered from 1 to 5. All sights and venues in the text have map references; eg, (3, H5) means Map 3, grid reference H5. See p96 for map symbols.

Prices

Multiple prices listed with reviews (eg €10/5) usually indicate adult/concession admission to a venue. Concession prices can include senior, student, member or coupon discounts. Meal cost and room rate categories are listed at the start of the Eating and Sleeping chapters, respectively.

Text Symbols

- ☎ telephone
- ✉ address
- ▣ email/website address
- € admission
- ☺ opening hours
- ⓘ information
- ⚓ vaporetto/traghetto stop
- 🚌 bus
- 🚆 train
- ♿ wheelchair access
- ✖ on-site/nearby eatery
- 👶 child-friendly venue
- Ⓥ good vegetarian selection

Best of Venice
3rd edition – January 2007
First published – June 2002

Published by Lonely Planet Publications Pty Ltd
ABN 36 005 607 983

Australia Head Office, Locked Bag 1, Footscray, Vic 3011
   ☎ 03 8379 8000, fax 03 8379 8111
   ▣ talk2us@lonelyplanet.com.au
USA 150 Linden St, Oakland, CA 94607
   ☎ 510 893 8555, toll free 800 275 8555
   fax 510 893 8572
   ▣ info@lonelyplanet.com
UK 72–82 Rosebery Ave, Clerkenwell, London
   EC1R 4RW
   ☎ 020 7841 9000, fax 020 7841 9001
   ▣ go@lonelyplanet.co.uk

This title was commissioned in Lonely Planet's London office and produced by: **Commissioning Editor** Paula Hardy **Coordinating Editor** Liani Solari **Coordinating Cartographer** Erin McManus **Coordinating Layout Designer** Jacqui Saunders **Managing Cartographer** Mark Griffiths **Assisting Editors** Anne Mulvaney, Alan Murphy **Assisting Cartographer** Matthew Kelly **Cover Designer** James Hardy **Project Manager** Sarah Sloane **Managing Editors** Gabrielle Wilson, Stephanie Pearson **Language Content Coordinator** Quentin Frayne **Mapping Development** Paul Piaia **Thanks to** Sally Darmody, Katie Lynch, Jennifer Garrett, Trent Paton, Celia Wood

© Lonely Planet Publications Pty Ltd 2007.

All rights reserved.

Photographs by Lonely Planet Images and Krzysztof Dydynski except for the following: p6, p16, p23, p41, p42, p43, p70, p80, p82 Juliet Coombe; p12 Roberto Soncin Gerometta; p13 Damien Simonis. **Cover photograph** Carpeted steps leading into canal, Monsoon Images/ Photolibrary. All images are copyright of the photographers unless otherwise indicated. Many of the images in this guide are available for licensing from Lonely Planet Images: www.lonelyplanetimages.com.

ISBN 978 1 74059 978 8
Printed through Colorcraft Ltd, Hong Kong.
Printed in China

Acknowledgments Venice Vaporetto Map © Actv S.p.A. 2006

Lonely Planet and the Lonely Planet logo are trademarks of Lonely Planet and are registered in the US Patent and Trademark Office and in other countries.

Lonely Planet does not allow its name or logo to be appropriated by commercial establishments, such as retailers, restaurants or hotels. Please let us know of any misuses: www.lonelyplanet.com/ip.

Contents

From the Publisher

AUTHOR
Damien Simonis

Damien is hooked. A first, brief encounter with this lady on the lagoon as a fresh-faced backpacker from the Antipodes left an indelible mark. He had to come back, it was just a question of when. Years later he finally did, amid a foul November squall and working for Lonely Planet. Things had changed in the meantime. Italian had become Damien's second language and he had since crisscrossed the bootlike Italian peninsula on assignment and off. What had been a near adolescent infatuation had now become something less ingenuous. Cracks began to appear beneath the make-up, but that only endeared him more to the place. As Damien learns to tread an ever finer path through the labyrinth of lanes (it's always fun to discover another shortcut!) and potter about in boats on the lagoon, our man in Venice can only confess to being hopelessly enamoured. Even when far away, he can still taste that slightly bitter afternoon *spritz* as the sun goes down.

Un grazie infinite a Luisa De Salvo (APT Venice) for all her enthusiasm and practical assistance. Yet again, Alberto Toso Fei, star journalist and city biographer, who wangled me onto his merry summer ship for some Redentore revelling; thanks to him and Olivia Alighieri. Many other people helped or were just plain good company along the way, including Irina Freguia, Caterina de Cesero and Francesco Lobina, Federica Rocco, Michela Scibilia, Federica Centulani, Antonella Dondi dall'Orologio, Lucialda Lombarda, Cristina Bottero (APT), and Alby and Francy who rocked up from Padua. *Mille grazie a tutti* for their time, help and companionship. Long may the flag of San Marco wave!

LONELY PLANET AUTHORS
Why is our travel information the best in the world? It's simple: our authors are independent, dedicated travellers. They don't research using just the internet or phone, and they don't take freebies in exchange for positive coverage. They travel widely, to all the popular spots and off the beaten track. They personally visit thousands of hotels, restaurants, cafés, bars, galleries, palaces, museums and more – and they take pride in getting all the details right, and telling it how it is. For more, see the authors section on **www.lonelyplanet.com**.

PHOTOGRAPHER
Krzysztof Dydyński

Born and raised in Warsaw, Poland, Krzysztof has travelled extensively across Europe, Asia and the Americas, writing and photographing for Lonely Planet for the past two decades. In the early 1990s he made Australia his new home but, like a migratory bird, has returned to Europe every year since, revisiting his favourite old cities and looking for new inspirations. Venice is one of his great loves in which to wander leisurely about a labyrinth of narrow lanes and tiny bridges, at dusk or dawn, savouring that unique, dreamlike place of grand palaces and countless canals.

SEND US YOUR FEEDBACK
We love to hear from travellers – your comments keep us on our toes and help make our books better. Our well-travelled team reads every word on what you loved or loathed about this book. Although we cannot reply individually to postal submissions, we always guarantee that your feedback goes straight to the appropriate authors, in time for the next edition – and the most useful submissions are rewarded with a free book. To send us your updates – and find out about Lonely Planet events, newsletters and travel news – visit our award-winning website: **www.lonelyplanet.com/feedback**.

Note: We may edit, reproduce and incorporate your comments in Lonely Planet products such as guidebooks, websites and digital products, so let us know if you don't want your comments reproduced or your name acknowledged. For a copy of our privacy policy visit **www.lonelyplanet.com/privacy**.

Introducing Venice

La Serenissima, as Venice is known, has often been anything but serene in its long and colourful history. Yet in many respects no term seems more fitting for this beguiling, enigmatic city. Unique in every way, Venice is more than a pretty place, it is a cast of mind and spirit.

Under siege by armies of tourists, the city and its people remain strangely unperturbed. As Venice floats in its lagoon sanctuary, so the Venetians waft by with an almost stealthy ease, as their forbears have done for centuries. Like any great beauty, it is at once admirable and elusive, almost a tease, but forever seductive.

Of course, Venice has always had its problems, from backbiting Byzantine politics to the perennial concerns of flooding and urban decay. The population has dropped by two-thirds since the 1950s. Paradoxically, real estate prices are sky-high as people from all over the world buy second residences, and something of an accommodation free-for-all sees new hotels and B&Bs popping up all the time. For some, the threat of Venice becoming one huge theme park is all too real.

Yet there is something of the phoenix about Venice, as though the sheer poetic power of its beauty were enough to maintain it exactly as it has been for another thousand years.

Venice is a festival of culture, a magnificent mosaic ranging from Romanesque and Veneto–Byzantine to Gothic and High Renaissance. Above all, Venice is a voyage of the imagination and a feast for the senses.

Dreamscape at dusk: Basilica di San Marco and the Campanile

Neighbourhoods

Seen from the air, Venice looks like a juicy slab of sole served up on a glittering platter, crossed with a dash of sauce in the shape of a reverse 's'. This is the *centro storico* (Venice proper), the core of the modern municipality of Venice, which covers the surrounding lagoon and islands (p34) and strips of the mainland.

The city has been divided into six *sestieri* (neighbourhoods) since the 12th century. Clockwise from the train station they are: Cannaregio, Castello, San Marco, Dorsoduro, San Polo and Santa Croce.

After the Grand Canal itself – the world's most romantic 'Main St' – one's thoughts turn to the central square, Piazza San Marco (p29), dominated by the sumptuous basilica (p9) and the Gothic Palazzo Ducale (p10), long the religious and political headquarters of the city. The *sestiere* around it, **San Marco**, is the heart of Venice chic and swarms with activity as visitors and locals converge on it for business, pleasure and shopping.

To the east sprawls **Castello**, once the furnace of Venetian industrial prowess centred on the Arsenale (p26) where la Serenissima's conquering fleets were built. It is a curious mix of workaday 'suburb' and, at its edge, residential tranquillity, full of agreeable distractions and home to the Biennale (p26).

Some of the city's greatest art treasures are held in collections in **Dorsoduro**, south over the Ponte dell'Accademia (p33), and the presence of the university gives it a fresh, young hum, particularly in the bars around Campo Santa Margherita. Separated from it by the Canale della Giudecca waterway lies the peaceful island haven of Giudecca (p34).

San Polo is gathered in around the Rialto markets (p51), long the centre of business and trade empire gossip, and now a minor focal point of nightlife. Its narrow lanes are crammed with boutiques and traditional eateries. Quieter is adjacent **Santa Croce**, whose western extremities have a grittier, portside feel. Opposite, **Cannaregio** is a feast of variety, from the Jewish Ghetto (p17) to the revelry of bars and restaurants around Fondamenta della Misericordia.

WALKING ON WATER

Living in Venice is like living in a fairy tale, but the daily routine presents its obstacles. Though there are no cars, getting to work can be equally frustrating when you find the streets packed with meandering visitors. The grocery shopping one can do is limited to what one can carry, and water taxis cost a fortune!

Itineraries

A walker's city, Venice can be tackled in countless meandering, exploratory forays. A **Museum Pass** (€18/12; valid 6 months) covers entry to a selection of the city's grand sights, including the Palazzo Ducale, Ca' Rezzonico and Ca' Pesaro. There are several variations on this pass.

FANFARE FOR THE FAITHFUL

Venice bristles with some of Italy's finest churches. A tour of the best would start at the Basilica di San Marco (p9), where across the Bacino di San Marco you can see the magnificent outline of Santa Maria della Salute (p23). Head east to San Zaccaria (p32) and then meander north to Santa Maria Formosa (p32) and on to the Gothic pile that is SS Giovanni e Paolo (p32), resting place of many a *doge* (duke). Nearby is the delicious Renaissance bijou of Santa Maria dei Miracoli (p32). From there a bit of a trek via the Rialto bridge would leave you admiring the art and architecture of Santa Maria Gloriosa dei Frari (p14).

> ### HIRE YOUR OWN BOAT
> To pootle about on your own, hire a motorboat from **Brussa** (4, B3; ☎ 041 71 57 87; www.brussaisboat.it; Fondamenta Labia, Cannaregio 331; per day €130; ⏰ 7.30am-5.30pm Mon-Sat, 7.30am-12.30pm Sun).

FOR ART'S SAKE

Art lovers will need to stake out their preferences. Starting at the Gallerie dell'Accademia (p12) for the classics, you quickly move to the city's main contemporary art show, the Peggy Guggenheim Collection (p13). Other key stops on the modern trail are Palazzo Grassi (p20) and Ca' Pesaro (p16). Much of Venice's classic art is still *in situ* in its churches and monuments. One of the most outstanding is the Scuola Grande di San Rocco (p15), a Tintoretto treasure house.

SS Giovanni e Paolo: resting place of many a *doge* (duke)

GET LOST!

Skirt the edges of the tourist flow. From the train station follow the crowd as far as Ponte delle Guglie and then head northwest along Canale di Cannaregio to the lagoon. Pass through residential areas and double-back east towards the Ghetto (p17). Stop for a bite along Fondamenta della Misericordia before crossing over into Castello, passing SS Giovanni e Paolo (p32) to arrive at the little visited San Francesco della Vigna (p30) and on to the Arsenale (p26). From there head deeper into the workaday Castello district, finally arriving at the distant, quiet Cattedrale di San Pietro (p30).

REASONS TO VISIT VENICE IN JANUARY *A Bluelist submitted by OneSmallBag*

A Relaxed Ambience The Venetians are more relaxed when their streets, transportation and eateries aren't besieged by tourists. You will be too.

More Economical High-priced hotels are willing to negotiate lower rates in January.

Bundle Up and Dine Alfresco January's frequent blue skies can make it pleasant to sit, if properly dressed against the cold, at outdoor cafés.

Keep the Olfactories Happy Pollution and heat can lead to unpleasant smells and sights in some of the canals during summer. This is much less of an issue in winter.

Save on Airfares In January, flights to Venice are often cheaper.

Every Ride is a Grand Cruise With more room on the *vaporetti* because of fewer tourists, every ride is a pleasure with easy viewing of the Grand Canal.

Avanti! Forget the queues for museums and galleries – stroll right in for uncrowded enjoyment of centuries of art and history.

Being Close is Easy For romantic closeness, bundled up and cuddly in winter can be infinitely preferable to hot and sticky in the swelter of summer.

Excuse Me, Excuse Me, Excuse Me… For photographers, the winter light has great appeal, as does the likelihood of photographs without a horde of other tourists in the frame.

www.lonelyplanet.com/bluelist

San Francesco della Vigna's façade packs a powerful Palladian punch

Highlights

BASILICA DI SAN MARCO (3, H4)

If you see one thing in Venice, this should be it. St Mark's Basilica, a cornucopia of untold artistic wealth, encapsulates in one location the glorious past and very marrow of the city's identity.

Consecrated in 1094 and built on a Greek-cross plan, the church embodies an utterly unique blend of styles, ranging from Byzantine and Romanesque to Gothic and Renaissance. Its five bulbous domes are strangely reminiscent of the mosques of Istanbul. In few places does East so marvellously blend with West.

INFORMATION

☎ 041 522 52 05
▢ www.basilicasanmarco.it
✉ Piazza San Marco, San Marco
€ Pala d'Oro €1.50; Tesoro (Treasury) €2; Galleria €3
🕑 9.45am-5.30pm Mon-Sat (closes 4.30pm Oct-Apr), 2-4pm Sun & hols
🚤 Vallaresso, San Marco & San Zaccaria
♿ limited
🍴 Caffè Quadri (p53)

DRESS CODE

You will not be allowed into the basilica wearing shorts (unless they cover the knees), and women must cover their shoulders and upper arms. You will also be refused entry with backpacks and big bags. These can be left for free (one-hour limit) at nearby **Ateneo di San Basso** (Calle San Basso; 🕑 9.30am-5.30pm), just off Piazzetta dei Leoni.

The story of the basilica is also one of theft: from the alleged body of St Mark, whisked away from Egypt, to the quadriga of bronze horses taken from Constantinople in 1204. The quadriga got around, as Napoleon whisked it off to Paris as booty after marching into the city in 1797. A copy of these four steeds bestrides the **Loggia dei Cavalli** above the main entrance. The originals are inside.

The arches above the main entrance boast fine mosaics, but they are nothing compared with the dazzling interior, coated in a shimmering layer of gold mosaics painstakingly created, repaired and completed over hundreds of years from the 11th century onward. The exquisite 12th-century marble pavement is an infinite variety of geometrical whimsy interspersed with floral and animal motifs.

Behind the altar is the **Pala d'Oro**, an exquisite gold-, enamel- and jewel-encrusted altarpiece made in Constantinople for Doge Pietro Orseolo I in 976 and added to over the centuries. Almost 2000 precious stones adorn it.

Sometimes all that glitters *is* gold

PALAZZO DUCALE (3, H5)

Welcome to the command centre of the Venetian Republic. The Doge's Palace, a rare example of civil Venetian Gothic, was home to the *doge* (duke) and all arms of government, including prisons. Two magnificent Gothic façades in white Istrian stone and pink Veronese marble face Piazzetta San Marco.

From the gallery atop these arches, the new *doge* would be proclaimed. He would stand at a point where the stone is darker, to contemplate executions in the piazzetta below. Inside, councils would meet and secret trials were held.

Established in the 9th century, the building began to assume

INFORMATION
- ☎ 041 271 59 11
- 🖳 www.museicivicivenezianiit
- ✉ Piazzetta San Marco 2, San Marco
- € €12/6.50 (incl Museo Correr, Museo Archeologico Nazionale & Biblioteca Nazionale Marciana)
- ☼ 9am-7pm Apr-Oct, 9am-5pm Nov-Mar
- ⓘ infrared radio receivers for loop commentary for hire (€6.50)
- ⚓ Vallaresso, San Marco & San Zaccaria
- ♿ fair
- 🍴 palace café

DON'T MISS
- Museo dell'Opera
- Veronese's paintings in the Sala del Consiglio dei Dieci
- Prigioni Nuove
- Itinerari Secreti (Secret Itineraries, a guided tour of lesser known parts of the palace, such as the Piombi where Casanova was imprisoned)

Glorious distractions in the meeting room of the Consiglio dei Dieci (Council of Ten)

its present form 500 years later. From the main courtyard, you ascend several stairways to reach the **Appartamento del Doge** (Duke's Apartments) and, upstairs another flight, the Halls of Power. The **Anticollegio** features four Tintorettos and the *Ratto d'Europa* (Rape of Europa) by Veronese. The ceiling of the **Sala del Collegio** features further works by both. Signs then lead you downstairs to the immense **Sala del Maggiore Consiglio** (Hall of the Grand Council), dominated by Tintoretto's *Paradiso,* one of the world's largest oil paintings.

A trail of corridors leads you to the **Ponte dei Sospiri** (Bridge of Sighs) that connects to the **Prigioni Nuove** (New Prisons) built on the east side of the canal to cater for overflow from the **Prigioni Vecchie** (Old Prisons) in the palace itself. Among the latter were the Piombi ('the Leads') in the roof, where legendary 18th-century philanderer Giacomo Casanova did some time.

GRAND CANAL (3)

Lord Byron rather liked swimming home to his apartments, after a nocturnal tryst, along this canal, Venice's 'Main St'. No-one would be so foolhardy today, but this busy thoroughfare in the form of an inverted 's' is a bazaar of colour, sound and smell, a timeless spectacle for the senses.

The 3.5km canal, which until late medieval times was a kind of river and port together, today supports an ever-changing parade of transport barges, *vaporetti* (water buses), water taxis, private speedboats, gondolas, police patrol boats, water ambulances and water fire brigade. This floating pageant is set against a backdrop of more than 100 grand *palazzi* (mansions) dating from the 12th to the 18th centuries.

INFORMATION

- ✉ Grand Canal
- € €5
- 🚉 No 1 stops all along the Grand Canal
- ♿ fair

Jump on the No 1 all-stops *vaporetto* at Piazzale Roma (3, A2) or Ferrovia (3, B1) for the half-hour meander along the world's most extraordinary traffic artery.

Just after the Riva de Biasio stop (4, B3) is the **Fondaco dei Turchi** (p24), recognisable by the three-storey towers on either side of its colonnade.

Past Rio di San Marcuola, the **Palazzo Vendramin-Calergi** (p28),

DON'T MISS

- Ca' Foscari (3, C4)
- Palazzo Grassi (3, D5)
- Palazzo Dario's marble façade (3, E6)
- Palazzo Corner (3, E6)

home of the casino, is on the left. To the right, just after the San Stae stop (3, E1), you'll see **Ca' Pesaro** (p16). Shortly after, to the left, is the **Ca' d'Oro** (p21), beyond which the boat heads toward the 16th-century **Ponte di Rialto** (p34) and bustling **Rialto Produce Markets** (p51).

The *vaporetto* sweeps on to the wooden **Ponte dell'Accademia** (p33), where you get off for the art gallery of the same name (p12), and on past the grand church of **Santa Maria della Salute** (p23) before reaching San Marco.

Iconic Venice: the Ponte di Rialto on the Grand Canal

GALLERIE DELL'ACCADEMIA (3, D6)

Long the official arbiter of artistic taste in Venice, the 'Academy' in this former church and convent is home to the single greatest collection of the finest in Venetian old masters, a veritable feast of High Renaissance, baroque and rococo. Although the city is dotted by works of the greats, this one-stop starburst represents a single, intense lesson in the greatness of Venetian high art.

INFORMATION

- ☎ 041 520 03 45
- 🖥 www.gallerieaccademia.org
- ✉ Campo della Carità, Dorsoduro 1050
- € adult/EU citizens 18-25/child under 12 & EU citizens under 18 & over 65 €6.50/3.25/free
- 🕑 8.15am-2pm Mon, 8.15am-7.15pm Tue-Sun
- ⓘ audioguide/videoguide €4/6
- 🚇 Accademia
- ♿ limited
- 🍴 Ai Gondolieri (p54)

In **Room 2**, Carpaccio's altarpiece, *Crocifissione e Apoteosi dei 10,000 Martiri del Monte Ararat* (Crucifixion and Apotheosis of the 10,000 Martyrs of Mt Ararat), is an extraordinary study in massacre and martyrdom. You stroll past works by the Bellinis, Mantegna and Cima da Conegliano until you are stopped in your tracks in **Room 5** by rare contribu-

DON'T MISS

- Tintoretto's *Assunzione della Vergine* and *Trafugamento del Corpo di San Marco*
- Tiepolo's *Castigo dei Serpenti*
- Art in the former Chiesa di Santa Maria della Carità
- Titian's *Presentazione di Maria al Tempio*

tions from Giorgione: *La Tempesta* (The Storm) and *La Vecchia* (The Old Woman). Both are centuries ahead of their time, the latter, in particular, presaging 19th-century portraiture.

Major works adorn **Room 10** and Paolo Veronese's *Convito in Casa di Levi* (Feast in the House of Levi) is one of the highlights. Also on display is one of Titian's last works, his disturbing *Pietà*.

Room 20 is a revelation. The crowd scenes, splashes of red and activity pouring from the canvases in the cycle dedicated to the *Miracoli della Vera Croce* (Miracles of the True Cross) are a vivid record of Venetian life by Carpaccio, Gentile Bellini and others.

Carpaccio's extraordinary series of nine paintings recounting the life of Santa Orsola, in **Room 21**, is the collection's last high point.

You can't go past a well-hung Venetian

PEGGY GUGGENHEIM COLLECTION (3, E6)

Eccentric millionaire art collector Peggy Guggenheim (1898–1979) called the unfinished **Palazzo Venier dei Leoni** home for 30 years. She left behind, apart from her 14 cherished dogs buried with her in the sculpture garden, a collection of works by her favourite modern artists, representing most of the major art movements of the 20th century. Money might not buy happiness, but it could certainly buy a helluva lot of spectacular art.

Most of the collection is in the **east wing**. Early Cubist paintings include Picasso's *Poet* (1911) and *Pipe, Glass, Bottle of Vieux Marc* (1914) and Georges Braque's *Clarinet* (1912). The list of greats is long

INFORMATION

- ☎ 041 240 54 11
- 🖥 www.guggenheim-venice.it
- ✉ Palazzo Venier dei Leoni, Dorsoduro 701
- € adult/senior/student & child €10/8/5
- ◔ 10am-6pm Wed-Mon
- ⓘ audioguide €5
- 🚉 Accademia
- ♿ good
- 🍴 museum café

A TIGHT FIST

The old adage about money and happiness rang true for Ms Guggenheim. According to one biographer, Anton Gill, she remained a lifelong penny-pincher despite amassing a fortune in modern art at bargain-basement prices. A regular at Harry's Bar, she apparently haggled over every bill. She died a lonely lady in her damp-plagued *palazzo*.

It's said that a lion was once kept in the garden of Palazzo Venier dei Leoni (lions)

and you'll want a couple of hours. Picasso's rival, Salvador Dalí, has some delirious contributions, like *Birth of Liquid Desires* (1932), and fellow Catalan Joan Miró chimes in with *Seated Woman II* (1939).

Among the many paintings by Max Ernst, Guggenheim's husband and doyen of Surrealism, is the disturbing *Antipope* (1942). Other names to look for include Jackson Pollock, Mark Rothko, Willem de Kooning, Paul Delvaux, Alexander Calder, Juan Gris, Kurt Schwitters, Paul Klee, Francis Bacon, Giorgio de Chirico, Piet Mondrian and Marc Chagall. Out in the **sculpture garden** are several curious pieces by, among others, Henry Moore and Alberto Giacometti. Yoko Ono contributed an olive 'wish tree' in 2003.

The rear of the mansion hosts a separate collection of Italian Futurists and works by other modern artists from the peninsula, including Giorgio Morandi, Giacomo Balla and Amedeo Modigliani. The west wing hosts temporary exhibitions.

SANTA MARIA GLORIOSA DEI FRARI (3, C3)

An exercise in elegant, sober majesty, this soaring Gothic temple was raised in brick for the Franciscan friars in the 14th and 15th centuries. A symbol of the order's power (matched by the equally imposing churches of its rivals, the Dominicans; in the case of Venice, by SS Giovanni e Paolo, p32), it is also a key stop on the art-lover's Venetian ramblings.

Although it may not look very Gothic to visitors accustomed to the style in its birthplace of France, the church's Latin-cross plan (with three naves and a transept), high vaulted ceiling and sheer size give it away.

The simplicity of the interior (red and white marble floor, with the same colours dominating the walls and ceiling) is offset by the extravagance of its decoration in the form of paintings and funereal monuments.

The mastery of **Titian** is the leitmotif of the Frari. His dramatic *Assunta* (Assumption; 1518), above the high altar, represents a key moment in his rise as one of the city's greatest artists, praised unreservedly by all as a work of genius.

Another of his masterpieces, the *Madonna di Ca' Pesaro* (Madonna of Ca' Pesaro), hangs above the Pesaro altar (in the left-hand aisle, near the choir stalls). Also of note are Giovanni Bellini's triptych, in the apse of the sacristy, and Donatello's statue of *Giovanni Battista* (John the Baptist), in the first chapel to the right of the high altar.

INFORMATION

- ✉ Campo dei Frari, San Polo 3004
- € €2.50 or Chorus ticket
- 🕐 9am-6pm Mon-Sat, 1-6pm Sun
- 🚉 San Tomà
- ♿ limited
- ✖ Frary's (p56)

CHORUS LINE

An organisation called **Chorus** (www.chorusvenezia.org) offers visitors a special ticket (€8/5, family ticket €16) providing entry to 15 outstanding churches. Entrance to individual churches is €2.50. Among the most striking are Santa Maria Gloriosa dei Frari, Santa Maria dei Miracoli, San Polo, Sant'Alvise, La Madonna dell'Orto, I Gesuati, San Pietro di Castello, Il Redentore and San Sebastian. The ticket, available from any of the churches, also includes the possibility of visiting the Tesoro (Treasury) in the Basilica di San Marco.

Inside Santa Maria Gloriosa dei Frari, where vertigo is next to godliness

SCUOLA GRANDE DI SAN ROCCO (3, C3)

Fans of Renaissance painter **Tintoretto** can gorge themselves on his work in one concentrated location, this *scuola* (religious confraternity) dedicated to St Roch.

Antonio Scarpagnino's (c1505–49) Renaissance **façade** (exhibiting a hint of the baroque to come), with its white marble columns and over-bearing magnificence, seems uncomfortably squeezed into the tight space of the narrow square below it. Either way, the real treat is inside.

After winning a competition to determine who would decorate

INFORMATION

☎ 041 523 48 64
🖳 www.scuolagrandesanrocco.it
✉ Campo San Rocco, Dorsoduro 3052
€ adult/18-26 yr old/child under 18 €7/5/free
🕙 9am-5.30pm Easter-Oct, 10am-5pm Nov-Easter
ⓘ audioguide included in ticket
🚇 San Tomà
♿ limited
🍴 Osteria San Pantalon (p55)

A MATTER OF SCHOOLING

The Scuola Grande di San Rocco was not, as the name might suggest, a 'big school'. It was, rather, one of six major religious confraternities in Venice, whose power and activities played a fundamental role in society. Attached to a church, these largely lay associations acted as parish community and welfare centres, and social clubs. Virtually all trade guilds also had small *scuole*, of which there were as many as 400.

The Sala Grande Superiore – treated to Tintoretto's mastery and Midas' touch

the school (Veronese was among his rivals), Tintoretto went on to devote 23 years of his life to this work. The more than 50 paintings by the master is altogether too much for the average human to digest in one swoop.

Chronologically speaking, you should start upstairs (Scarpagnino designed the staircase) in the **Sala Grande Superiore**. Here you can pick up mirrors to carry around and so avoid a sore neck while inspecting the ceiling paintings, which depict Old Testament episodes. Around the walls are scenes from the New Testament. Other artists (such as Titian, Giorgione and Tiepolo) also managed to sneak a handful of works in. To give your eyes a rest from the paintings, inspect the woodwork below them – it is studded with curious designs, including a false book collection.

Downstairs, the walls of the confraternity's **assembly hall** feature a series on the life of the Virgin Mary, starting on the left wall with the *Annunciazione* (Annunciation) and ending with the *Assunzione* (Assumption) opposite.

CA' PESARO (3, E1)

For some, Venice has a bit of a stick-in-the-mud image, but here is bundled one of the city's key modern art collections together with possibly one of the city's most intriguing museums, dedicated to Asian art and artefacts. All this is housed in one of the finest of the city's grand patrician houses standing proud on the Grand Canal.

INFORMATION

- ☎ 041 524 06 95
- 🖥 www.museiciviciveneziani.it
- ✉ Fondamenta de Ca' Pesaro, Santa Croce 2076
- € €5.50/3
- 🕙 10am-6pm Tue-Sun Apr-Oct, 10am-5pm Tue-Sun Nov-Mar
- 🚋 San Stae
- ♿ limited
- ✕ Vecio Fritolin (p58)

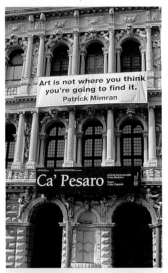

DON'T MISS

- Auguste Rodin's *Il Pensatore* (The Thinker)
- Kandinsky's *Tre Triangoli* (Three Triangles)
- The classic *terrazzo alla veneziana* floors, typical of Venetian mansions
- The Indonesian shadow puppet collection

Built to a design by Longhena in muted baroque fashion, the house was completed in 1710. It has known several owners down through the centuries. In the old days, guests of the Pesaro family would arrive in style at the Grand Canal entrance. We humbler visitors come through the sunny rear courtyard and find ourselves in the *androne,* the hangar-like ground floor hall, decorated with a few sculptures and other exhibits.

The **Galleria d'Arte Moderna** (Modern Art Gallery), which includes works purchased from the Biennale art festival, begins upstairs with late 19th-century Venetian artists (such as Giacomo Favretto with scenes from Venice) and other Italians.

International contributions include works by Klimt, Kandinsky, Chagall, Henri Matisse, Paul Klee and Spain's Joaquim Sorolla. Next come striking sculptures by the Milanese Adolfo Widt and the eclectic De Lisi collection, with works by De Chirico, Miró and Yves Tanguy. Max Ernst, Henry Moore and others feature in a room dedicated to the 1940s and '50s.

Upstairs is the intriguing **Museo d'Arte Orientale**, one of the most important collections in Europe of Edo-period art and objects from Japan. It includes armour, weapons, porcelain, artworks and countless household objects, as well as material from elsewhere in Asia.

GHETTO (4, C1 & B2)

The idea of concentrating Jews into specific parts of the city was pan-European and has its roots in at least the Middle Ages. But the modern universal word to describe such quarters comes from Venice.

The first records of Jews in Venice (Ashkenazi of German and Eastern European origin) date to the 10th century. In 1516 all were ordered to live in the area around the Getto Novo (New Foundry). The Ashkenazis' pronunciation gave us the word 'ghetto'.

Free to move around the city by day if they wore a yellow cap or badge, the Jews were locked in behind the gates of the Getto Novo at midnight.

The ghetto was tiny, and over-crowding turned the buildings around Campo di Ghetto Nuovo into 'mini-skyscrapers' – some apartment blocks have seven storeys, with low ceilings. Atop three were built modest *schole* (synagogues). The **Schola Tedesca** (German Synagogue) is above the building that houses the **Museo Ebraico** (Jewish Museum; ☎ 041 71 53 59; www.museoebraico.it;

INFORMATION
- 🖳 www.ghetto.it
- ✉ Campo di Ghetto Nuovo, Cannaregio 2902/b
- € €8.50/7 for tour of ghetto & Museo Ebraico
- 🏛 Guglie
- ♿ limited
- ✖ Gam Gam (p59)

Campo di Ghetto Nuovo

Campo di Ghetto Nuovo, Cannaregio 2902/b; ☽ 10am-7pm Sun-Fri Jun-Sep, 10am-4.30pm Sun-Fri Oct-May). Virtually next door is the **Schola Canton** (Corner Synagogue) and further around is the **Schola Italiana**, the simplest of the three.

In 1541 waves of Sephardi Jews from Spain and Portugal arrived, many of them wealthy merchants, and the town authorities ceded another small area, the Getto Vecio (Old Foundry), or Ghetto Vecchio. Here they built two beautiful synagogues, the **Schola Spagnola** and the **Schola Levantina**, on Campiello delle Schole. The half-hourly to hourly **guided tours** (☽ 10.30am-5.30pm Sun-Fri, except Jewish holidays) are recommended.

THE JEWS OF VENICE

Until around 1553 Venice's Jewish community thrived. Its trade was welcome and the community built a reputation for book printing. Then Pope Julian banned such activities and things went downhill. In 1797 Napoleon abolished restrictions on Jews and by 1866 all minorities had been guaranteed equality. In 1943 many of Venice's 1670 Jews were interned and some 200 wound up in Nazi death camps. Only a handful remain in the ghetto today.

BURANO (5, F1)

From afar they could be the product of a child's imagination and the primary colours of a Lego building-block set. The bright pastel-coloured houses of the north lagoon fishermen's island are its call sign (while its star product remains lace). The bonbon colours have their origin in the fishermen's desire to see their houses when heading home from a day at sea.

INFORMATION

- 🏛 Burano
- ♿ limited
- 🍴 Al Gatto Nero

Given the island's distance from Venice (it takes about 40 minutes by ferry), the feeling of having arrived somewhere only fleetingly touched by la Serenissima is inescapable; Burano has a deep quietude.

The **Museo del Merletto** (☎ 041 73 00 34; www.museiciviciveneziani .it; Piazza Galuppi 187; €4/2.50; ☉ 10am-5pm Wed-Mon Apr-Oct, 10am-4pm Wed-Mon Nov-Mar) is Burano's lace-making museum. The islanders became famous for their lace in the late 19th century after the long-moribund industry was resuscitated. If you buy lace on the island, choose with care, as much of the cheaper stuff is now factory produced and imported.

If you make the effort to visit (most people take in Murano and Torcello on the same trip), try to give yourself time to wander into the quietest corners and shady parks. Cross the wooden bridge to neighbouring **Mazzorbo** (which has its own *vaporetto* stop), a larger island with a few houses, a couple of trattorias and open green space. A snooze in the grass takes you light years from the monumental overdose of Venice.

A STITCH IN TIME

Venetian lace was a much sought-after commodity from the 15th century onwards, but was eclipsed by French production in the 18th century. The industry was saved from extinction when lace schools were founded on the island of Burano, largely to alleviate poverty, at the end of the 19th century. One still occasionally sees women stitching away on doorsteps and in parks today.

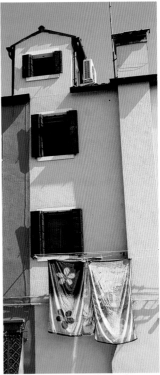
Burano homes: a perennial colourfest

TORCELLO (5, E1)

Long ago largely abandoned to nature, it is difficult to imagine Torcello bustling with 20,000 early medieval inhabitants; the descendants of those fled the mainland before the barbarian invasions at the twilight of the Roman Empire. It is perhaps easier to imagine Hemingway here in the aftermath of WWII, duck-hunting by day and boozing and writing by night.

Less than a 10-minute walk from the *vaporetto* stop lies the square around which huddles what remains of old Torcello – the lasting homes of the clergy and the island's secular rulers when it was the seat of the bishopric of mainland Altinum (Altino).

INFORMATION
- ☎ 041 270 24 64 (cattedrale)
- ✉ Torcello
- € cattedrale €3; bell tower €3; incl Museo di Torcello €8
- ◷ 10.30am-6pm Mar-Oct, 10am-5pm Nov-Feb
- ⓘ audioguides for mosaics in cathedral
- 🚊 Torcello
- ♿ limited
- ✕ Locanda Cipriani (p74)

The **Cattedrale di Santa Maria Assunta** was founded in the 7th century and was Venice's first – this was then the leading lagoon settlement. What you see of the church today dates from its first expansion in 824 and rebuilding in 1008. The three apses (the central one dates from the original structure) have a Romanesque quality.

The magnificent **Byzantine mosaics** inside, dating from the 12th and 13th centuries, are fascinating.

DON'T MISS
- ● Chiesa di Santa Fosca
- ● Palazzo del Consiglio
- ● Museo di Torcello

On the western wall is a vast mosaic depicting the Last Judgment. Hell (lower right side) does not look any fun at all. The greatest treasure is the mosaic of the Madonna in the half-dome of the central apse. Starkly set on a pure gold background, the figure is one of the most stunning works of Byzantine art you will see in Italy.

It is also possible to climb the **bell tower**, from which you'll be greeted by great views across the island and lagoon.

Byzantine magnificence: stunning mosaic of the Madonna in Venice's oldest cathedral

PALAZZO GRASSI (3, D5)

Magnates can be a mercurial lot. French wheeler-dealer and contemporary art collector François Pinault surprised just about everyone in France and Italy when he snapped up the grand Palazzo Grassi in Venice as the central home for his considerable and eclectic collection.

Palazzo Grassi is named after the family that commissioned its grand, classical design from Giorgio Massari (1687–1766) in 1749. It is built around a classical, enclosed colonnaded courtyard. For more than 40 years, until 2005, it had been the centre of temporary exhibitions, and since 1984 in the

INFORMATION
- ☎ 041 523 16 80
- 🖥 www.palazzograssi.it
- ✉ Campo San Samuele, San Marco 3231
- € €10/6
- 🕙 10am-7pm
- ℹ tickets can be acquired online at www.vivaticket.it with €1 commission
- 🚣 San Samuele
- ♿ good
- 🍴 Palazzo Grassi Café

FRANCE'S WOUNDED GRANDEUR

'Eternity is the time of art, not of those projects designed to serve it,' magnate François Pinault remarked tartly in early 2005 when he announced he was dropping long-stalled plans to open an art and cultural centre in a former Renault car factory at Ile Seguin, northern France. He denounced interminable bureaucratic delays and switched his plans to Venice, which for once moved with unaccustomed celerity to close this deal. The French have still not recovered from this *gifle*.

Contemplating the past, present and future of Palazzo Grassi

hands of troubled car-marker Fiat. Fiat sold up and Pinault stepped in, snapping up an 80% share of the building for the bargain price of €29 million. Given a light-handed (and mostly reversible) contemporary overhaul on the inside by star Japanese architect Tadao Ando, the Pinault art HQ is set to become one of the city's, and Europe's, cultural beacons. Overhaul work continues on the *teatrino*, a little private theatre which will become an auditorium for cultural events.

A part of Pinault's vast possessions (more than 2000 items) is often (for instance, throughout 2006 and 2007), but not always, on rotating display in temporary themed exhibitions lasting around six months. Other planned exhibitions include a major Picasso retrospective from late 2006 and another on Rome and the Barbarians in 2008. Pinault's collection covers a broad canvas of modern and contemporary art, including such modern icons as Mark Rothko, Jeff Koons, Mario Merz and Cy Twombly.

CA' D'ORO (3, F1)

This magnificent 15th-century Gothic structure got its name (Golden House) from the gilding that originally decorated the façade's sculptural details. Visible from the Grand Canal, the ornate Gothic façade (even without the shimmering gold) stands out from the rest of the edifice, which seems drab by comparison.

All that glitters is not necessarily gold, and inside Ca' d'Oro are all sorts of other jewels: an impressive collection of bronzes, tapestries and paintings that constitutes the **Galleria Franchetti**.

INFORMATION

- ☎ 041 523 87 90 or booking 041 520 03 45
- 🖳 www.cadoro.org
- ✉ Calle di Ca' d'Oro, Cannaregio 3931
- € €5/2.50
- 🕒 8.15am-2pm Mon, 8.15am-7.15pm Tue-Sun
- ℹ audioguide €4
- 🚊 Ca' d'Oro
- ♿ limited
- 🍴 Osteria dalla Vedova (p59)

THIRST FOR FAME

Of the many well heads scattered across the city (many of them of great artistic beauty), only three can be ascribed to a particular sculptor: those inside the Palazzo Ducale and the one in Ca' d'Oro, by Bartolomeo Bon (c1410–67), a celebrated sculptor and architect in late Gothic Venice.

Inimitable façade of Venice's Golden House

The 1st floor is devoted mainly to religious painting, sculpture and bronzes from the 15th and early 16th centuries. One of the first items you'll see is a polyptych recounting the martyrdom of San Bartolomeo (St Bartholomew). The violence is remarkable, as is the saintly indifference with which Bartholomew accepts his torment! Much of what you see on this floor is Venetian, but one room has been set aside for Tuscan art.

On the 2nd floor you can see a series of fragments of frescoes saved from the outside of the Fondaco dei Tedeschi (p27), an important German trading house that is now home to the central post office. All but one are by Titian. The other, a nude by Giorgione, is the most striking. Also on this floor is a mixed collection, including works by Tintoretto, Carpaccio, Mantegna, Vivarini, Titian, Signorelli and Van Eyck.

A big incentive for visiting is the chance to lean out over the Grand Canal from the balconies on the 1st and 2nd floors.

SAN GIORGIO MAGGIORE (2, F5)

One might almost feel that Palladio's church of San Giorgio Maggiore (on the island of the same name) should be the city's opera house. Rising seemingly straight from the waters of the lagoon, it is deliberately theatrical and looks like a grand set when observed from across the water.

Built between 1565 and 1580, it is Palladio's most imposing structure in Venice, although it inspired as many catcalls as cheers when completed. The **façade**, erected the following century, is believed to conform with the architect's plan. The massive columns on high plinths, crowning tympanum and statues contain an element of sculptural chiaroscuro, casting strong shadows and reinforcing the impression of strength.

San Giorgio Maggiore's **art treasures** include Tintoretto's *Ultima Cena* (Last Supper) and the *Raccolta della Manna* (Shower of Manna), on the walls of the high altar, and a *Deposizione* (Deposition) in the Cappella dei Morti. Take the lift to the top of the 60m-high **bell tower** for an extraordinary view.

INFORMATION

- ☎ 041 522 78 27
- ✉ San Giorgio Maggiore, Giudecca
- € free, bell tower €3
- ☼ 9.30am-12.30pm & 2.30-6.30pm (closes 4.30pm Oct-Apr)
- 🚉 San Giorgio
- ♿ limited

The stage is set...

Behind the church spread the grounds of the former monastery. Established in the 10th century by the Benedictines, it was rebuilt in the 13th century and expanded over the 16th century, and finished with the magnificent library built by Longhena in the 1640s. You can visit the library, cloisters and grounds, all now part of the cultural foundation, **Fondazione Cini** (☎ 041 524 01 19; www.cini.it; adult/senior & child 7-12/child under 7 €12/10/free; ☼ 10am-4.30pm Sat-Sun by 1hr guided visit only).

VENICE IN THE MOVIES

Agent 007 returns to Venice in Martin Campbell's *Casino Royale* (2006), the latest Bond blockbuster, with scenes in Piazza San Marco, at Riva del Vin on the Grand Canal, the Giudecca (near Hotel Cipriani) and more. Shots from Michael Radford's *The Merchant of Venice* (2005), with Al Pacino, include the Ponte di Rialto and Ghetto, while *Casanova* (2005), starring Heath Ledger, was shot all over town, including Piazza San Marco, Campo dei Frari and Riva degli Schiavoni. They are the latest in a long line of films shot in Venice. The **Associazione Culturale VeniceMarcoPolo** (☎ 320 979 77 74; Via dello Squero, 50, Mestre) runs two-hour cinema-location walking tours.

SANTA MARIA DELLA SALUTE (3, F6)

Baldassare Longhena's dazzling white monolith is arguably the city's most familiar silhouette – viewed from Piazzetta San Marco (3, H5) or the Ponte dell'Accademia (3, D6).

Longhena received a commission to build the church in honour of the Virgin Mary, who, it was believed, delivered the city from an outbreak of plague in 1630. The ranks of statues that festoon the exterior of the church culminate in one of Our Lady atop the dome.

Longhena's idea was to design it in the form of a crown for the mother of God, hence its unusual, octagonal form. More extraordinary is that it is built on a bed of pylons jammed into the lagoon. The cavernous interior is flooded with light pouring through windows in the walls and dome. Dominating the main body of the church is the baroque **altar maggiore** (high altar), with an icon of Mary brought to Venice from Crete.

The **sacristy** ceiling is bedecked with three remarkable works by Titian. The figures depicted are so full of curvaceous movement they seem to be caught in the spin cycle of a washing machine! The three scenes are replete with high emotion, showing the struggles between Cain and Abel (*Caino e Abele*), David and Goliath (*David e Golia*) and, finally, Abraham and his conscience (*Il Sacrificio di Isaaco*; The Sacrifice of Isaac). Take a close look at Titian's medallions of several saints, whose lively facial expressions seem anything but saintly.

INFORMATION

- ☎ 041 274 39 28
- 💻 www.marcianum.it/salute
- ✉ Campo della Salute, Dorsoduro 1/b
- € sacristy €1.50
- 🕑 9am-noon & 3.30-6pm
- 🚤 Salute
- ♿ limited
- ✗ Linea d'Ombra (p54)

A THANKSGIVING BRIDGE

Every year, on 21 November, a procession takes place from Piazza San Marco to the Santa Maria della Salute church to give thanks for the city's deliverance from a bout of plague in 1630. The last part of the march takes place on a pontoon bridge thrown out between the Santa Maria del Giglio *traghetto* (commuter gondola) stop and the church.

Our Lady's 'crown', built in honour of the city's deliverance from plague in 1630

Sights & Activities

MUSEUMS & GALLERIES

Ca' Rezzonico – Museo del Settecento Veneziano (3, C5)

Poet Robert Browning, no doubt mesmerised by the Grand Canal views, drew his last breath in this Longhena-designed baroque noble mansion. Today it is a vast museum of the 18th century, with art and furniture of a magnificent bygone age. Particularly noteworthy is Tiepolo's ceiling fresco in the Sala del Trono (Throne Room). The Salone da Ballo (Ballroom) drips with frescoes and is richly furnished.
☎ 041 241 01 00 ☐ www .museicivicivenezani.it ✉ Fondamenta Rezzonico, Dorsoduro 3136 € adult/student/child €6.50/4.50/2.50 ☼ 10am-6pm Wed-Mon Apr-Oct, 10am-5pm Wed-Mon Nov-Mar ⚓ Ca' Rezzonico ♿ good

Fondaco dei Turchi (3, D1)

Once the seat of the Turkish trading community in Venice (who remained until 1858), this 12th-century pile today houses the curious Museo Civico di Storia Naturale (Natural History Museum), partially open to the public. The main display consists of remains of an Ouransaurus and a 12m-long prehistoric crocodile skeleton found by an Italian expedition in the Sahara in the 1970s.
☎ 041 275 02 06 ☐ www .museicivicivenezani.it ✉ Salizada del Fondaco dei Turchi, Santa Croce 1730 € free ☼ 9am-1pm Tue-Fri, 10am-4pm Sat & Sun ⚓ Riva de Biasio & San Stae ♿ good

Museo Correr (3, G5)

Having ripped down a church at the west end of Piazza San Marco, Napoleon built what became known as the Napoleonic wing to house his Venetian ballroom, however there's no dancing around the dense display of 19th-century paintings, books, documents, model galleys, maps, weaponry and other Venetian paraphernalia in here. Attached is the Museo Archeologico, crammed with Greek and Roman statuary, and the Libreria Nazionale Marciana, with its 16th-century Sala della Libreria, a grand reading room decorated by, among others, Veronese.
☎ 041 240 52 11 ☐ www .museicivicivenezani.it ✉ Piazza San Marco, San Marco 52 € €12/6.50 (incl Palazzo Ducale) ☼ 9am-7pm Apr-Oct, 9am-5pm Nov-Mar ⚓ San Marco & Vallaresso ♿ fair

Museo d'Arte Erotica (3, G4)

What was once one of the great pleasure domes of Europe now has a museum dedicated to erotic art. Over four floors in Palazzo Rota, a tasteful collection of art from Venice and beyond, past and present, explores the pleasures of the body. A section is dedicated to, well, who else but Casanova?
☎ 041 520 39 00 ☐ www .museodarteerotica.com ✉ San Marco 834 € €10/6 ☼ 10am-11pm ⚓ San Marco & Vallaresso

Dripping with decadence: Ca' Rezzonico's ballroom

Royal barge in the Museo Storico Navale (the lion's open book denotes peacetime)

Museo della Fondazione Querini-Stampalia (3, J3)

From the outside it seems the umpteenth-centuries-old Venetian noble family mansion, which it is, but inside it features some surprising modern touches by Venetian architect Carlo Scarpa. The Querini family left behind a treasure of furniture, minor art and gewgaws. Most curious of all are Gabriele Bella's scenes of Venetian life.
☎ 041 271 14 11 ▱ www .querinistampalia.it ✉ Ponte Querini, Castello 4778 € €6/4 ◷ 10am-6pm Tue-Thu & Sun, 10am-10pm Fri & Sat ⛴ San Zaccaria ♿ limited

Museo delle Icone (2, F4)

Many of the intriguing icons on show here were done by Greeks in Venice and northern Italy after the fall of Byzantium. Foremost exceptions are two 14th-century Byzantine icons, one representing Christ in Glory and the other the Virgin Mary with Child and Apostles. Attached to San Giorgio dei Greci (p31), this gallery is a unique haven of Orthodox religious art and a symbol of Venice's religious tolerance.
☎ 041 522 65 81 ▱ www .istitutoellenico.org ✉ Campiello dei Greci, Castello 3412 € €4/2 ◷ 9am-12.30pm & 1.30-4.30pm Mon-Sat, 9am-5pm Sun ⛴ San Zaccaria

Museo Diocesano d'Arte Sacra (3, J4)

The charming Romanesque cloister, a rarity in Venice, is the main attraction here. The display of religious art and objects is housed upstairs in rooms of the former Benedictine monastery dedicated to Sant'Apollonia. Hours are extended and entry charged for temporary exhibitions.
☎ 041 522 91 66 ✉ Fondamenta di Sant'Apollonia, Castello 4312 € voluntary contribution ◷ 10.30am-12.30pm Mon-Sat ⛴ San Zaccaria

Museo Storico Navale (2, G5)

Spread over four floors in a former grain silo, this museum traces the maritime history of the city and Italy. Models abound of everything, from the *bucintoro* – the *doges'* (dukes') ceremonial barge – to WWII battleships. On the 3rd floor are moored a few gondolas, including Peggy Guggenheim's.
☎ 041 520 02 76 ✉ Fondamenta dell'Arsenale, Castello 2148 € €1.55 ◷ 8.45am-1.30pm Mon-Fri, 8.45am-1pm Sat ⛴ Arsenale

Palazzo Fortuny (3, E4)

Eccentric Spanish painter and collector Mariano Fortuny y Madrazo bought this Gothic townhouse, which sports two rows of *hectafores*, each a series of eight connected Venetian-style windows, in the early 20th century. His works, and another 80 by the Roman artist Virgilio Guidi, make up the core of the display, still not entirely open to the public.
☎ 041 520 09 95 ▱ www .museicivicveneziani.it ✉ Campo San Beneto, San Marco 3780 € €4/2.50 ◷ 10am-6pm Tue-Sun ⛴ Sant'Angelo

Palazzo Franchetti (3, D6)

This magnificent 16th-century *palazzo* (palace) is the scene of major temporary exhibitions. From the entrance off the campo, a grand

19th-century staircase winds up to the noble 1st floor, where the exhibitions are held. A series of magnificent halls, especially the central one and the three overlooking the Grand Canal, form the stage for exhibitions.
☎ 041 240 77 11 🖳 www
.istitutoveneto.it ✉ Campo Santo Stefano, San Marco 2842 € €7/5 🕑 2-7pm Mon-Sat, 11am-7pm Sun & hols 🚤 Accademia 🚲 fair

Telecom Future Centre (3, G3)
Callboxes to the future line the hallowed walkways of a 15th-century cloister. Only in a place like Venice could the national telephone company install its local HQ and museum in such a seemingly timeless setting. Steeped in the past in the cloister of the adjacent church of San Salvador (p31), you get interactive with telephones and other gizmos that show us how we might communicate in years to come.
☎ 041 521 32 00 🖳 www
.futurecentre.telecomitalia
.it ✉ Campo San Salvador, San Marco 4826 € free
🕑 10am-6pm Tue-Sun
🚤 Rialto

NOTABLE BUILDINGS & MONUMENTS

Arsenale (2, G4)
Dante envisaged it almost as a scene from hell, with boiling black pitch and infernally industrious cacophony. For centuries Venice ruled the seas, churning out its merchant ships and warships in these now hushed shipyards. Founded in 1104,

the site is navy property but the Biennale has taken over parts to stage exhibitions and theatre (p69).
✉ Campo del'Arsenale, Castello 2407 € depends on exhibition 🕑 depends on exhibition 🚤 Arsenale

Ateneo Veneto (3, F5)
This learned society, founded in Napoleon's time, has its residence in what was long the headquarters of the confraternity of San Girolamo and Santa Maria della Giustizia. Its members' main task was to accompany criminals on death row in their last moments, hence the building was known as the Scuola 'dei Picai' (the old Venetian version of Dead Men Walking).
✉ Campo San Fantin, San Marco 🚤 Vallaresso & San Marco 🚲 limited

Bartolomeo Colleoni Statue (3, J2)
Verrocchio, the Florentine Renaissance genius of sculpture, was charged with creating this magnificent equestrian statue of the *condottiero* Bartolomeo

Watchful eye on the Arsenale

Colleoni (1400–76), a mercenary warrior long in Venice's pay from 1448. He bequeathed his considerable wealth to the Republic on condition that his statue be raised in Piazza San Marco. Venice took the money but was less than honest about carrying out Colleoni's wishes to the full.
✉ Campo SS Giovanni e Paolo, Castello 🚤 Ospedale Civile

Biennale Internazionale d'Arte (2, H5)
Every year the east end of Venice fills up with art and architecture buffs for the Biennale extravaganza, and its pavilions form a mini-

---

INSIDER VIEW: FRESCOES WORTH MORE THAN A THOUSAND WORDS

Ca' Rezzonico (p24) holds *the* masterpiece by Giandomenico Tiepolo (1727–1804), the frescoes he did for his villa at Zianigo. Tiepolo, Giambattista's third son and a visionary in times of great change, did the frescoes from 1759 to 1797. They reveal much about his attitudes. We witness the futile attempts of man to create for himself an ultimately vain story, an illusory drama of gestures, grimaces, greatness and misery in which mythological beasts, monsters and heroes live, die and search for inexistent answers, amid the vacuousness of fops and the uncertainty of history.

Monica da Cortà Fumei, Marketing & Communications Director, Musei Civici Veneziani

INSIDER VIEW: A FRENCHMAN IN VENICE

I would recommend two monuments that symbolise perfectly Venice's historical diversity and unique acceptance of foreign cultures. At the Cattedrale di San Pietro di Castello (p30), whose façade Palladio designed in 1558, admire the Coranic quotations engraved in the 'bishop's throne'. Near Rialto, you go to buy stamps at the main post office and unexpectedly step into the Fondaco dei Tedeschi (below), once the headquarters of German merchants, with its Renaissance courtyard, three orders of *loggie* (galleries) and refined Byzantine crenellation. I've never posted so many letters in my life!

Jean-Jacques Aillagon, Director of Palazzo Grassi

compendium of 20th-century architectural thinking that can be seen any time. Carlo Scarpa worked on the Italian pavilion and built the Venezuelan one (1954). Equally curious are the Padiglione del Libro (Book Pavilion; 1991) and the Dutch (1954), Austrian (1934) and Australian (1988) pavilions. ✉ Biennale Internazionale d'Arte, Castello 🚢 Giardini ♿ good

Casa di Goldoni (3, D3)
Venice's greatest playwright, Carlo Goldoni (1707–93), was born in Palazzo Centani, now better known simply as his house. Its intriguing courtyard with fountain and staircase in Istrian stone will draw you in, although there is little to see in the museum itself but some 18th-century marionettes and a series of images of, and commentaries (in Italian) on, the playwright.
☎ 041 275 93 25 🖳 www .museiciviciveneziani .it ✉ Calle Nomboli, San Polo 2794 € €2.50/1.50 🕐 10am-5pm Mon-Sat Apr-Oct, 10am-4pm Mon-Sat Nov-Mar 🚢 San Tomà ♿ good

Dogana da Mar (3, G6)
The Punta della Dogana is like the prow of a Venetian galley, carving a path between

the Grand Canal and the Canale della Giudecca. Atop the Dogana da Mar (former customs) buildings are two bronze Atlases, above which turns capricious Fortune, an elaborate weather vane. Capricious indeed, but long frustrated plans to convert the buildings into a modern art gallery may finally get the go-ahead in late 2006. The hot money is on French magnate François Pinault, whose enormous collection (see Palazzo Grassi, p20) would find a perfect home in this major space.
✉ Punta della Dogana, Dorsoduro 10 🚢 Salute ♿ good

Fondaco dei Tedeschi (3, G2)
Picture this now somewhat dour pile resplendent in bright frescoes by Giorgione

and Titian. What is now merely a post office was from the 13th century the nerve centre of the German business community. The present *fondaco* (trading house) was raised after a fire in 1505.
✉ Salizada del Fondaco dei Tedeschi, San Marco 5346 🕐 8.30am-6.30pm Mon-Sat 🚢 Rialto ♿ good

Magazzini del Sale (2, D5)
These centuries-old warehouses for the city's stocks of salt (a prized commodity in the days before refrigeration) have been carefully restored for use as exhibition space, partly for a future gallery of Venetian artist Emilio Vedova's legacy of works. Salt has so deeply penetrated the lower walls over the years that it acts as a glue and can't be removed!

Magnificent but misplaced: statue of Bartolomeo Colleoni

We can only assume the Ospedaletto's charges were well behaved

✉ Fondamenta delle Zattere, Dorsoduro 258-266 🚊 Zattere

Oratorio dei Crociferi (2, E3)

In this little gem across the road from the grand Gesuiti church is a tiny 12th-century oratory, once part of a hospice. In the 16th century Palma il Giovane was hired to plaster the walls with paintings and frescoes.
☎ 041 532 29 20
✉ Campo dei Gesuiti, Cannaregio 4095 € €2
⌚ 3.30-6.30pm Fri-Sat Apr-Oct 🚊 Fondamente Nuove

Ospedaletto (2, F4)

They look down at you like somewhat miffed deities, these outsized baroque sculptures leaning out over the narrow *calle* (street) from the walls of Longhena's 17th-century 'Little Hospital' (aka the church of Santa Maria dei Derelitti). The church is annexed to what was a hospice and orphanage. Inside you can see the elegantly frescoed Sala da Musica, where female orphans performed concerts.

☎ 041 532 29 20 ✉ Barbaria delle Tole, Castello 6691 € €2 (Sala da Musica) ⌚ 3.30-6.30pm Thu-Sat Apr-Oct, 3-6pm Thu-Sat Nov-Mar 🚊 Ospedale Civile

Palazzo Contarini del Bovolo (3, F4)

Like an X-ray of a mini Leaning Tower of Pisa (without the lean), a dizzying external spiral (*bovolo* in the Venetian dialect) staircase is the centrepiece of this late 15th-century Contarini family mansion. It is tucked down a back lane from where the staircase is visible if you don't wish to pay to climb it.
☎ 041 532 29 20 ✉ Calle Contarini del Bovolo, San Marco 4299 € €3.50 ⌚ 10am-6pm Apr-Oct, 10am-4pm Sat & Sun Nov-Mar 🚊 Rialto ♿ limited

Palazzo Dario (3, E6)

Catch the No 1 *vaporetto* (p37) to admire the best profile of this *palazzo* – the unique Renaissance marble facing. The place is supposed to be cursed, as several of its owners over the years

have succumbed to sudden and sometimes unpleasant deaths. Film-maker Woody Allen is just one prospective owner put off by its reputation.
✉ Calle Barbaro, Dorsoduro 352 🚊 Salute

Palazzo Mocenigo (3, E1)

Once the property of one of the Republic's most important families, this mansion now houses a modest museum featuring period clothes, furnishings and accessories of the 18th century. This is how the other half lived in the twilight years of la Serenissima.
☎ 041 72 17 98 🖥 www .museicivicieneziani.it ✉ Salizada di San Stae, Santa Croce 1992 € €4/2.50 ⌚ 10am-5pm Tue-Sun Apr-Oct, 10am-4pm Tue-Sun Nov-Mar 🚊 San Stae

Palazzo Vendramin-Calergi (4, D3)

Gamblers approaching by *motoscafo* (water taxi) get some sense of how composer Richard Wagner must have felt when arriving by gondola

to take up temporary residence here. Little did he know that he would never leave, dying in this very building in 1883. His rooms are open to the public on Saturday morning only by guided visit (which you must book on Friday from 10am to noon). Otherwise, if you don a jacket, you can try your luck in the casino too (p67).
☎ 349 593 69 90
✉ Campiello Vendramin, Cannaregio 2040 € €5
☺ 10.30am Sat ♨ San Marcuola ♿ limited

Piazza San Marco (3, H5)
The glorious bellybutton of Venice, St Mark's Square is fronted by the basilica and other emblematic buildings like the Procuratie Nuove, the Procuratie Vecchie, the Ala Napoleonica (with the Museo Correr, p24), the now re-stored **Torre dell'Orologio** (clock tower; ☎ 041 522 49

A LOPSIDED LOOK
Making a good gondola is no easy task – seven different types of wood are employed to make 280 pieces for the hull alone, which *must* be asymmetrical. The left side has a greater curve to make up for the lateral action of the oar, and the cross section is skewed to the right to counterbalance the weight of the gondolier.

51; visits possible by prior arrangement), the **Campanile** (€6/3; ☺ 9.45am-8pm Jul-Sep, 9.30am-5pm Apr-Jun, 9.45am-4pm Oct-Mar) and the basilica's freestanding bell tower, from the top of which you can enjoy breathtaking views.
✉ Piazza San Marco, San Marco ♨ Rialto ♿ limited

Scuola di San Giorgio degli Schiavoni (2, F4)
Take a close look at the image of St George dispatching the dragon (with bits of its human victims scattered about) to the next life on

---

the ground floor. It is one of a series of superb paintings by Vittore Carpaccio depicting events connected with Dalmatia's three patron saints: George, Tryphone and Jerome. Dalmatia (in modern Croatia) was long faithful Venetian territory, and Venice's Dalmatian community established this religious school in the 15th century.
☎ 041 522 88 28 ✉ Calle dei Furlani, Castello 3259/a € €3 ☺ 9.30am-12.30pm & 3.30-6.30pm Tue-Sat, 9.30am-12.30pm Sun Apr-Oct, 10am-12.30pm & 3-6pm Tue-Sat, 10am-12.30pm Sun Nov-Mar ♨ San Zaccaria ♿ limited

Scuola Grande dei Carmini (3, B5)
In its heyday, this was probably the most powerful of Venice's religious confraternities, with a membership in 1675 of 75,000. The façades have been attributed to Longhena. Seek out the nine splendid ceiling paintings by Tiepolo upstairs in the Salone Superiore. They depict the virtues surrounding the Virgin in Glory.
☎ 041 528 94 20 ✉ Campo Santa Margherita, Dorsoduro 2617 € adult/student/child €5/4/2 ☺ 9am-6pm Mon-Sat, 9am-4pm Sun Apr-Oct, 9am-4pm Nov-Mar ♨ Ca' Rezzonico ♿ limited

Palazzo Contarini del Bovolo's dizzying spiral staircase

Squero di San Trovaso
(3, C6)
On the leafy banks of the Rio di San Trovaso, one of Venice's most attractive waterways, survives one of the city's few working *squeri* (gondola workshops). From the right bank, observe vessels in various states of (dis)repair in the timber sheds.
⊠ Campo San Trovaso, Dorsoduro 1097 🚤 Zattere

Teatro La Fenice (3, F5)
The magnificently if somewhat tardily resurrected opera house, rebuilt after fire in 2003, is one of the world's great stages. If you can't make a show, it's possible to visit by day. Book ahead by phone (☎ 041 24 24). You will be told when booking at what time on what days a tour in your language is available.
☎ 041 78 66 11 🖥 www
.teatrolafenice.it ⊠ Campo San Fantin 1965 € €7/5 (guided tour) 🕑 varies
🚤 Santa Maria del Giglio

CHURCHES & CATHEDRALS

Cattedrale di San Pietro di Castello (2, H4)
This isolated, tranquil, post-Palladian cathedral accompa-

nied by a gleaming, leaning bell tower is the latest in a long line of churches that have stood here since 775. Although Venice's cathedral until 1807, for centuries it had been bridesmaid to the Basilica di San Marco.
⊠ Isola di San Pietro, Castello € €2.50 or Chorus ticket 🕑 10am-5pm Mon-Sat 🚤 San Pietro

Gesuati (2, D5)
Also known as the Chiesa di Santa Maria del Rosario, this 18th-century Dominican church contains ceiling frescoes by Tiepolo telling the story of St Dominic. The statues lining the interior are by Gian Maria Morlaiter (1699–1781).
☎ 041 523 06 25 ⊠ Fondamenta Zattere ai Gesuati, Dorsoduro 918 € €2.50 or Chorus ticket 🕑 10am-5pm Mon-Sat 🚤 Zattere
♿ limited

I Gesuiti (2, E3)
The Jesuits took over this church in 1657 and reconstructed it in Roman baroque style. Inside, the lavish décor includes white and gold stucco, white and green marble floors, and flourishes filling empty slots. Remarkable

paintings include Tintoretto's *Assunzione della Vergine* (Assumption of the Virgin) and Titian's *Martirio di San Lorenzo* (Martyrdom of St Lawrence).
☎ 041 528 65 79 ⊠ Campo dei Gesuiti, Cannaregio 4885 € free 🕑 10am-noon & 4-6pm 🚤 Fondamente Nuove
♿ limited

Madonna dell'Orto (4, E1)
This was Tintoretto's parish church, and he left his mark in no uncertain fashion. Among his frescoes are the *Giudizio Finale* (Last Judgement), *Adorazione del Vitello d'Oro* (Adoration of the Golden Calf) and *Presentazione di Maria al Tempio* (Presentation of the Virgin Mary in the Temple). Tintoretto is buried with other family members in the church.
⊠ Campo della Madonna dell'Orto, Cannaregio 3520 € €2.50 or Chorus ticket 🕑 10am-5pm Mon-Sat 🚤 Madonna dell'Orto
♿ limited

San Francesco della Vigna (2, F4)
The first glimpse of this powerful Palladian façade comes as a shock. The church itself was designed by Sansovino for the Franciscans on the site of a vineyard. The bell tower could be the twin of St Mark's Campanile. Inside, the Cappella dei Giustiniani, left of the main altar, is decorated with splendid reliefs by Pietro Lombardo and his school.
⊠ Campo San Francesco della Vigna, Castello 2787 € free 🕑 8am-12.30pm & 3-7pm 🚤 Celestia
♿ limited

I Gesuiti: theatrical on the outside, lavish on the inside

San Giacomo dell'Orio
(3, D1)
Built to replace a 9th-century church (in 1225), this is one of the few decent examples of Romanesque in Venice. The main Gothic addition (14th century) is the remarkable wooden ceiling. Among the intriguing jumble inside you'll find a 13th-century baptismal font, a Byzantine column in green marble and a rare work by Lorenzo Lotto, *Madonna col Bambino e Santi* (Madonna with Child and Saints).
⊠ Campo di San Giacomo dell'Orio, Santa Croce
€ €2.50 or Chorus ticket
🕑 10am-5pm Mon-Sat
🚊 Riva de Biasio 🚻 limited

San Giorgio dei Greci
(2, F4)
Here in 1536 Greek Orthodox refugees were allowed to raise a church. It is interesting for the richness of its Byzantine icons, iconostasis and other works inside. Visit the Museo delle Icone (p25) next door.
☎ 041 523 95 69 ⊠ Campiello dei Greci, Castello 3412 € free 🕑 9.30am-12.30pm & 2.30-5pm Mon & Wed-Sat, 9.30am-12.30pm Sun 🚊 San Zaccaria

San Giovanni Elemosinario (3, F2)
Half hidden by houses, this tiny Renaissance church is easily missed. Inside, the highlights are Pordenone's dome frescoes and another by Titian.
⊠ Ruga Vecchia San Giovanni, San Polo 477
€ €2.50 or Chorus ticket
🕑 10am-5pm Mon-Sat
🚊 Rialto

Madonna dell'Orto: Tintoretto's parish church

San Polo (3, E3)
Largely obscured by the housing tacked onto it, you'd never know this church is of Byzantine origin. Even less obvious is that inside a whole cycle by Tiepolo, the *Via Crucis* (Stations of the Cross), awaits scrutiny!
⊠ Campo San Polo, San Polo 2118 € €2.50 or Chorus ticket 🕑 10am-5pm Mon-Sat 🚊 San Silvestro 🚻 limited

San Salvador (3, G3)
Titian is the key player in this church laid out on a plan of three Greek crosses laid end to end. Look out in particular for his *Annunciazione* (Annunciation) and, behind the main altar, the *Trasfigurazione* (Transfiguration).

☎ 041 523 67 17 🖥 www .chiesasansalvador.it
⊠ Campo San Salvador, San Marco 4835 € free
🕑 9am-noon & 3-6pm Mon-Sat Apr-Oct, 9am-noon & 4-6pm Mon-Sat Nov-Mar
🚊 Rialto 🚻 limited

San Sebastian (3, A5)
This is the Renaissance reconstruction of Paolo Veronese's parish church. The artist filled the interior with frescoes and canvases that cover much of the ceiling and walls. The organ is his work too, with scenes from Christ's life on its shutters. Titian contributed *San Nicolò*, on the right as you enter.
⊠ Campo San Sebastiano, Dorsoduro € €2.50 or Chorus ticket 🕑 10am-5pm Mon-Sat 🚊 San Basilio 🚻 limited

PONTOON PILGRIMS
On the third Saturday of July each year, a grand pontoon bridge is created from all sorts of boats tied together between the Zattere (from outside Spirito Santo) and the church of SS Redentore (p33), allowing the citizens of Venice to make a pilgrimage their forebears first undertook in 1578. Many people hang about on the boats with friends to party and watch the fireworks that night. The Festa del Redentore (Feast of the Redeemer) remains one of the city's prime celebrations.

Santa Maria dei Miracoli – don't forget to step inside

San Stae (3, E1)

The busy baroque façade of this church dedicated to St Eustace (San Stae) belies the simple interior. Among its art treasures are Tiepolo's *Il Martirio di San Bartolomeo* (the Martyrdom of St Bartholomew). Next door, to the left (No 1980), is the Scuola dei Tiraoro e Battioro, the former seat of the goldsmith confraternity's *scuola* (school).
✉ Campo San Stae, Santa Croce 1979 € €2.50 or Chorus ticket ⏰ 10am-5pm Mon-Sat ⚓ San Stae ♿ limited

San Zaccaria (2, F4)

Construction of this church started in Gothic (see the apses) but ended in Renaissance. On the second altar to the left after you enter is a startlingly vivid image of the Virgin Mary by Giovanni Bellini. The Cappella di Sant'Atanasio holds some Tintorettos and Tiepolos, and the vaults of the Cappella di San Tarasion are covered in frescoes.
☎ 041 522 12 57
✉ Campo San Zaccaria, Castello 4693 € free,

Cappella di Sant'Atanasio €1 ⏰ 10am-noon & 4-6pm Mon-Sat, 4-6pm Sun ⚓ San Zaccaria ♿ limited

Santa Maria dei Miracoli (3, H2)

Well might one speak of *miracoli* (miracles). Pietro Lombardo was responsible for this Renaissance jewel, carapaced inside and out in marble bas-reliefs and statues. The timber ceiling is also eye-catching. Pietro and Tullio Lombardo executed the carvings on the choir.
✉ Campo dei Miracoli, Cannaregio 6074 € €2.50 or Chorus ticket ⏰ 10am-5pm Mon-Sat ⚓ Rialto ♿ limited

Santa Maria del Giglio (3, F5)

The baroque façade features maps of European cities and hides the fact that a church has stood here since the 10th century. A small affair, it is jammed with paintings, such as Peter Paul Rubens' only work in Venice, *Madonna col Bambino e San Giovanni* (Virgin Mary with Child and St John).
✉ Campo Santa Maria Zobenigo, San Marco 2543 € €2.50 or Chorus ticket ⏰ 10am-5pm Mon-Sat ⚓ Santa Maria del Giglio ♿ limited

Santa Maria Formosa (3, J3)

Rebuilt in 1492 on the site of a 7th-century church, the name Santa Maria Formosa stems from the legend behind the church's initial foundation. San Magno, bishop of Oderzo, is said to have had a vision of the Virgin Mary on this spot. In

this instance she was *formosa* (beautiful, curvy). Inside is an altarpiece by Palma il Vecchio depicting St Barbara.
✉ Campo Santa Maria Formosa, Castello 5254 € €2.50 or Chorus ticket ⏰ 10am-5pm Mon-Sat ⚓ San Zaccaria ♿ limited

Sant'Alvise (2, D2)

Built in 1388, this church hosts a noteworthy Tiepolo, the *Salita al Calvario* (Climb to Calvary), a distressingly human depiction of one of Christ's falls under the weight of the cross. The ceiling frescoes are a riot of colour.
✉ Campo Sant'Alvise, Cannaregio 3205 € €2.50 or Chorus ticket ⏰ 10am-5pm Mon-Sat ⚓ Sant'Alvise ♿ limited

Santo Stefano (3, E5)

Santo Stefano boasts the finest timber ceiling of any church in Venice. In the museum, right of the altar, is a collection of Tintorettos, including the *Ultima Cena* (Last Supper) and *Lavanda dei Piedi* (Washing of the Feet). The bell tower has a worrying lean!
✉ Campo Santo Stefano, San Marco 3825 € free; museum €2.50 or Chorus ticket ⏰ 10am-5pm Mon-Sat ⚓ Accademia ♿ limited

SS Giovanni e Paolo (3, J2)

Known also as San Zanipolo in Venetian, this grand Dominican Gothic church was completed in 1430 and rivals the Franciscans' Santa Maria Gloriosa dei Frari (p14). A ducal pantheon with 25 *doges'* tombs, it is a vast place full of curios. Peep into the Cappella del Rosario, off the north arm of the tran-

THE OLDEST PROFESSION

In the 1530s Venice had about 11,000 registered prostitutes of a population of 120,000. In the late 15th century a city ordinance stipulated that ladies of the night should hawk bare-breasted. La Serenissima was concerned that its men were increasingly turning to sodomy. Fearing for Venetian manhood, prostitution was encouraged and sodomy made punishable by death. Veronica Franco, one of the city's best known courtesans, didn't need to prowl the *calli* for business. Poet, friend of Tintoretto and lover of France's King Henry III, Miss Franco's costly services were in a class of their own and ranged from witty discourse to horizontal folk dancing.

sept, for some masterpieces by Paolo Veronese. The 15th-century rose window in the transept is a masterpiece.
☎ 041 523 59 13 ⊠ Campo SS Giovanni e Paolo, Cannaregio €€2.50 ☀ 9.30am-6pm Mon-Sat, 1-6pm Sun 🚢 Ospedale Civile ♿ fair

SS Redentore (2, D6)

A bout of plague in 1577 caused much death and panic, and its passing was such a relief that Venice's authorities ordered Palladio to design this grand church in thanksgiving. Antonio da Ponte finished the job. Its powerful, theatrical façade is best viewed from a distance.
⊠ Campo del SS Redentore, Giudecca 94 €€2.50 or Chorus ticket ☀ 10am-5pm Mon-Sat 🚢 Redentore ♿ limited

BRIDGES

Ponte dei Scalzi (3, B1)

This elegant, high-arched stone bridge is the first of the three (soon to be four) across the Grand Canal. Built in 1934, it replaced an iron bridge built by the Austrians in 1858.

⊠ Ponte dei Scalzi, Cannaregio/Santa Croce 🚢 Ferrovia

Ponte dell'Accademia (3, D6)

Built in timber in 1930 to replace a 19th-century metal structure, the third and last of the Grand Canal bridges was supposed to be a temporary arrangement. From the middle, the views

both up and down the Grand Canal are spellbinding.
⊠ Ponte dell'Accademia, Dorsoduro/San Marco 🚢 Accademia

Ponte delle Guglie (4, B2)

So-called because of the *guglie* (little obelisks) at either end, this is the main crossing point over the Canale di Cannaregio, and there probably isn't a tourist who doesn't use it en route from the train station to Piazza San Marco – as a tollway it would be a money-spinner!
⊠ Ponte delle Guglie, Cannaregio 🚢 Guglie ♿ fair

Ponte delle Tette (3, E2)

Tits Bridge got its name around the late 15th century because prostitutes around here displayed their wares to encourage business. Beyond the bridge is Rio Terà delle Carampane. The name came

Sensible pedestrians look to the right *and* left when crossing Ponte dell'Accademia

ROW YOUR BOAT

Back in 1882 the **Reale Società Canottieri Bucintoro** (☎ 041 520 56 30; www.bucintoro.org; Dorsoduro 15) was established by royal concession. Inspired by the English rowing fraternities of Oxbridge, the club furnished Italy with Olympic champions and today boasts about 300 members. Outsiders are welcome to join. Even rank beginners can have a go at learning to row, either *voga veneta* (the local standing version) or the classical sit-down style known here as *voga inglese* (English rowing). Courses start from €30 for an hour of one-on-one tuition. A rival club, **Canottieri Giudecca** (☎ 041 528 74 09; www.canottierigiudecca.com; Fondamenta del Ponte Lungo, Giudecca 259), also offers rowing courses (€6 an hour per person for group lessons). Either way, it's a wonderful way to get a different perspective on the lagoon.

from a noble family's house (Ca' Rampani), and at some point the ladies of the night who loitered here also came to be known as *carampane*.

✉ Ponte delle Tette, San Polo 🚊 San Stae

Ponte di Calatrava (3, A2)

A rare flash of modernity is being added, albeit slowed by the Byzantine meanderings of Venetian politics, to the Venetian cityscape with Santiago Calatrava's bridge, a fantasy of glass, stone and steel that is being built to link Piazzale Roma with the train station.

✉ Ponte di Calatrava, Santa Croce/Cannaregio

🚊 Piazzale Roma & Ferrovia

Ponte di Rialto (3, G3)

For centuries the only bridge over the Grand Canal was here, linking the Rialto with San Marco. Antonio da Ponte (Anthony of the Bridge) completed this robust marble version in 1592, at a cost of 250,000 ducats. To see what one of its predecessors looked like, view the cycle of painting dedicated to the Miracles of the True Cross in room 20 of the Gallerie dell'Accademia (p12).

✉ Ponte di Rialto, San Polo/San Marco 🚊 Rialto

ISLANDS

Giudecca (2, A6-E6)

Lying like a long outer sea wall south of Venice, the tranquil island of Giudecca was a favourite holiday-home location for Venice's great and good, before becoming the site of factories, boatyards and prisons in the 19th century, which can't have done anything for property prices. Big names like Elton John have again turned the tables. The main attraction is Palladio's church of SS Redentore (p33).

✉ Giudecca 🚊 Sacca Fisola, Redentore & Zitelle

Le Vignole (5, E2)

The southwest of Le Vignole is owned by the military and contains an old seaward fort, Forte Sant'Andrea, which may one day be opened to the public. The island long produced the bulk of the *doges'* wine, and its 50 or so inhabitants still live mainly from agriculture.

✉ Le Vignole 🚊 Vignole ♿ limited

Lido (5, E3)

On summer weekends Venetians flock to the beach here (the best of them are at the south end) and in September celebs from all over crowd in to the Palazzo della Mostra del Cinema for the Venice Film Festival (see Special Events, p63). At the north end of this long wisp of an island is the Antico Cimitero Israelitico (former Jewish cemetery), which can be visited by organised tour – ask at the Museo Ebraico (see Ghetto, p17).

✉ Lido 🚊 Lido ♿ limited

Ponte di Rialto and the lull of gentle waves – welcome to Venice

Lobsters are a specialty on Lido in summer

Murano (2, G1)
Venetians have been making crystal and glass since the 10th century. The bulk of the industry was moved to Murano in 1291 and production methods were a closely guarded secret. Look out for glassworks along Fondamenta dei Vetrai and Viale Garibaldi. The **Museo Vetrario** (2, H1; ☎ 041 73 95 86; Fondamenta Giustinian 8; €5.50/3 🕙 10am-6pm Thu-Tue Apr-Oct, 10am-5pm Thu-Tue Nov-Mar) has some exquisite pieces. The church of **SS Maria e Donato** (Campo San Donato; free; 🕙 9am-noon & 3.30-7pm Mon-Sat, 3.30-7pm Sun) is a fascinating example of Veneto-Byzantine architecture.
✉ Murano 🚊 Colonna, Faro & Museo 🚹 limited

Pellestrina (1, D3)
Pellestrina stretches south like the edge of an 11km-long razor blade from the Lido to Chioggia. Small villages of farming and fishing families (with a handful of good seafood eateries) are spread out along the island, protected on the seaward side by the Murazzi (sea walls), a feat of 18th-century engineering.
✉ Pellestrina 🚊 Lido & No 11 bus 🚹 limited

San Francesco del Deserto (5, F1)
The Franciscans built a monastery on this island 1km south of Burano to keep away from it all. Legend says Francis of Assisi himself landed here. Malaria and other hardships obliged the Franciscans to leave in 1420 but Pope Pius II subsequently granted the island to another order, the **Minori Osservanti** (☎ 041 528 68 63; donation encouraged 🕙 9-11am & 3-5pm Tue-Sun), that has stuck it out to this day.
🖳 www.isola-sanfrancesco deldeserto.it ✉ San Francesco del Deserto 🚊 water taxi from Burano 🚹 limited

San Lazzaro degli Armeni (5, D3)
The Armenian Mechitarist fathers were not squeamish about taking over this former leper colony in 1717. They set to work founding a monastery and an important centre of learning. Visitors can see the 18th-century refectory, church, library, museum and **art gallery** (☎ 041 526 01 04; €6/3; 🕙 guided tour only 3.25-5pm), along with a room dedicated to Lord Byron, who frequently stayed on the island when not tangling with the fairer sex in Venice.
✉ San Lazzaro degli Armeni 🚊 San Lazzaro 🚹 limited

San Michele (2, F2)
Napoleon established this island cemetery away from the city for health reasons and the church of San Michele in Isola was among

Mosaic on a tomb in the cemetery, San Michele

you can see the Torre Massimiliana, a 19th-century Austrian defensive fort in the southeast.

✉ Sant'Erasmo 🚢 Capannone, Chiesa & Punta Vela 🚻 limited

VENICE FOR CHILDREN

Art and architecture might not keep the kids amused for long but there is plenty of interesting activity on the city's waterways. A *gelato* (ice cream) at strategic intervals works wonders. You cannot avoid the bridges, so leave the pram at home and invest in a baby backpack.

the city's first Renaissance buildings. Ezra Pound, Sergei Diaghilev and Igor Stravinsky are pushing up daisies here, in the 'acatholic' sections.

✉ San Michele € free 🕐 7.30am-4pm Oct-Mar, 7.30am-6pm Apr-Sep 🚢 Cimitero 🚻 limited

San Servolo (5, D3)
The focal point of what was once an island madhouse is the Museo della Follia (Museum of Madness), two intriguing rooms full of paraphernalia and explanations of the days when being sent to San Servolo was undesirable. Of particular interest is the ancient pharmacy, where for centuries many of Venice's medicines were concocted. The guided tour of the island, which must

be booked in advance, also takes in the park and modest church.

☎ 041 524 01 19 ✉ San Servolo € free 🕐 phone bookings 9.30am-5.30pm Mon-Thu, 9.30am-3.30pm Fri 🚢 San Servolo

Sant'Erasmo (5, E2-F2)
Together with Le Vignole, Sant'Erasmo was long known as the *orto di Venezia* (Venice's garden) and its 1000 inhabitants remain largely dedicated to rural pursuits. Apart from green fields, quiet settlements and a couple of summertime restaurants,

Giardini Pubblici (2, G5)
The city's most extensive public park is a trifle tatty, but it's better than nothing and you will find swings and things to amuse the bairns. A handy restaurant/bar with outdoor seating completes the picture.

✉ Giardini Pubblici, Castello 🚢 Giardini 🚻 fair

Gondola Rides
Once the standard means of getting around town, these strangely shaped vessels remain for many the quintessence of romantic Venice. They are as enchanting for wide-eyed kids as starry-eyed lovers! You can hire

FOR KIDS OF ALL AGES
• Museo Storico Navale (p25)
• Campanile (see Piazza San Marco, p29)
• Telecom Future Centre (p26)

Parents can hear themselves think on the *vaporetto* No 1

them for tours or even as taxis if you have lots of cash.
☎ 041 528 50 75 € €73 for 50 min before 8pm, €91 after 8pm

Lido Beaches (5, E3)
In summer the beach is a winner. Getting there involves a soothing ferry ride to the Lido and then either walking to nearby pay beaches or getting a bus or rental bicycle to look for free beaches further south (such as at Alberoni).
✉ Lido € €5-10 to rent sun lounges on some beaches
🚣 Lido ♿ limited

Parco Savorgnan (4, A2)
You'd hardly know this quiet park existed unless directed there. It is a small affair but has swings and diversions for the kids and can come as welcome relief from the chaos in the railway station area.
☎ 041 521 70 11 ✉ Fondamenta Savorgnan, Cannaregio 🕐 8am-5.30pm Oct-Mar, 8am-7.30pm Apr-Sep 🚣 Guglie ♿ good

Vaporetto No 1
This one is a must for all the family. Hop aboard the all-stops No 1 *vaporetto* from your arrival point (for most this is the train station or

Piazzale Roma) and chug along the Grand Canal. It's a trip kids aged one to 100 can do time and again.
🚣 No 1 ♿ limited

COURSES

Bottega del Tintoretto (4, E1)
Roberto Mazzetto is one of the last printers in Venice to keep this once flourishing craft alive. He runs courses in printing, art and design, including five-day intensive summer courses.
☎ 041 72 20 81 💻 www .tintorettovenezia.it
✉ Fondamenta dei Mori, Cannaregio 3400 € 5-day course €360

Ca' Macana (3, C5)
This well-known mask-maker (see p47) runs short courses (2½ hours each) in mask-making and mask decorating, usually for groups of at least 10. The bigger the group, the less it costs per head. After the decorating course, you take home your own mask. It was planned to cater for smaller groups (with classes on Wednesday and Friday at around €50 per person) from late 2006. Check the website.

☎ 041 522 97 49 💻 www .camacana.com ✉ Calle delle Botteghe, Dorsoduro 3172 € up to €60

Delicious Italy (3, F6)
Held in special rooms of the Hotel Gritti Palace, these three-day cooking courses are theme-based and limited to a maximum of 16 participants. You can arrange full packages including accommodation in the hotel.
☎ 041 79 46 11 💻 www .deliciousitaly.com/venice cookingcourses.htm ✉ Hotel Gritti Palace, Campo Santa Maria del Giglio, San Marco 2467 € €680

Istituto Venezia (3, C4)
This school offers one-week courses (or longer) in all levels of Italian language. It also offers one-on-one tuition by the hour. In addition, the school runs combined language and art courses. Prices depend on the nature and intensiveness of the courses.
☎ 041 522 43 31 💻 www .istitutovenezia.com
✉ Campo Santa Margherita, Dorsoduro 3116/a € per week €160-540

RiViviNatura (3, E5)
This association offers daily Venetian cooking classes for a maximum of six people. You learn the secrets in the preparation of local dishes, in a private attic apartment, then sample the results. An optional add-on is going on a shopping run to the Rialto Markets.
☎ 041 296 07 26 💻 www .rivivinatura.it ✉ Calle dei Vitturi, San Marco 2923
€ per person €50

Trips & Tours

WALKING & BOAT TOURS
Rambling to the Rialto

Start by the church of **SS Giovanni e Paolo** (**1**; p32) and the **Scuola Grande di San Marco** (**2**). Pass below the statue of **Bartolomeo Colleoni** (**3**; p26) as

Paintings of prophets, patriarchs and saints adorn Santa Maria dei Miracoli's interior

you cross the bridge and head west for the church of **Santa Maria dei Miracoli** (**4**; p32). From its entrance proceed southeast across the Rio di San Marina and swing westwards – you will see the **Teatro Malibran** (**5**) as you make for the church of **San Giovanni Crisostomo** (**6**) before turning south past the grim-looking **Fondaco dei Tedeschi** (**7**; p27) for **Campo San Bartolomeo** (**8**). After saluting Goldoni's statue, go west for Venice's emblematic bridge, the **Ponte di Rialto** (**9**; p34), which leads to the area of the same name. Once the financial hub of Venice, it is a crush of activity as people flock to the markets. On your right is the Renaissance **Palazzo dei Camerlenghi** (**10**) and just beyond that the church of **San Giacomo di Rialto** (**11**). To your left is the **Palazzo dei Dieci Savi** (**12**; Palace of the Ten Wise Men). In its shadow stands the **Fabbriche Vecchie** (**13**). Passing the **Fabbriche Nuove** (**14**) you finish at the 700-year-old **Pescaria** (**15**; Fish Market; p50), rebuilt in 1907. Pop into All'Arco (p55) for traditional snacks and refreshments.

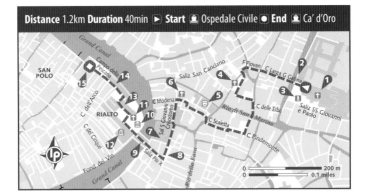

Pushing the Boat Out

Those with day or multi passes for lagoon transport can really push the boat out and get away from the crowds of San Marco. Start with the quick crossing from Fondamente Nuove, via the cemetery island of **San Michele** (**1**; p35), to **Murano** (**2**; p35), where the highlights are watching glass-blowers and visiting the Museo Vetrario. From Murano, head to **Burano** (**4**; p18) – you could get off at sleepy **Mazzorbo** (**3**) on the way and continue on foot over the bridge. On Burano, wander past the perkily painted houses and watch the lace-makers before haggling for a private boat to the **Isola di San Francesco del Deserto** (**5**; p35) and its monastery. Back at Burano, pick up the boat for

Glass blower at the Fornace CAM, Murano

peaceful **Torcello** (**6**; p19), where a meal at Locanda Cipriani (p74) might be in order. This itself makes a full day, but there's more, best done on a separate day, for those who thought it impossible to get off the beaten track in Venice. From Fondamente Nuove (or Burano via Treporti) make for the big, tranquil isle of **Sant'Erasmo** (**7**; p36), great for quiet strolls or bicycle rides (hire is possible, with luck, at the modest Il Lato Azzurro hotel, www.latoazzurro.it), and neighbouring **Le Vignole** (**8**; p34), home of the San Andrea fort and with a wild and woolly feel.

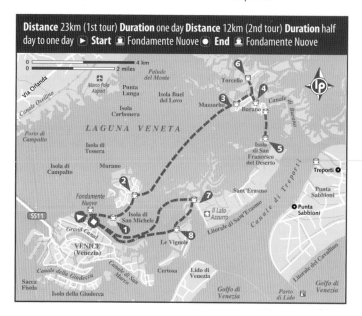

Distance 23km (1st tour) **Duration** one day **Distance** 12km (2nd tour) **Duration** half day to one day ▶ **Start** 🚢 Fondamente Nuove ⬤ **End** 🚢 Fondamente Nuove

Between Cathedrals

This takes us from the Basilica di San Marco to the church it usurped as cathedral, San Pietro. Begin at **Piazza San Marco** (**1**; p29), where you could while away hours. Turn into Piazzetta di San Marco and pass between the statue-symbols of Venice, St Theodore and St Mark (represented by the lion). Turn east. On the first bridge look north to the **Ponte dei Sospiri** (Bridge of Sighs; **2**) and duck up Calle degli Albanesi for the **Museo Diocesano d'Arte Sacra** (**3**; p25) and its Romanesque cloister. Go east along Salizada San Provolo to the church of **San Zaccaria** (**4**; p32), from whose square you return to the waterfront. The lagoonside stroll takes you past **La Pietà** (**5**), Vivaldi's church, to the **Museo Storico Navale** (**6**; p25). A small detour will take you to the once mighty **Arsenale** (**7**; p26). An excellent nearby lunch stop is Trattoria Corte Sconta (p60). Back by the water, swing inland along Castello's main drag, Via G Garibaldi, where you plunge into local life and could stop for a drink in one

Oh, to be held captive in Venice (sigh...)

of the cafés before dropping south through the **Giardini Pubblici** (**8**; p36). Sidle north alongside residential Sant'Elena and back to Via G Garibaldi. Proceed to the **Cattedrale di San Pietro di Castello** (**9**; p30) on the eponymous island.

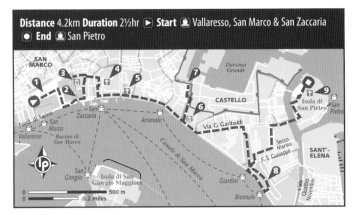

Distance 4.2km **Duration** 2½hr ▶ **Start** 🚊 Vallaresso, San Marco & San Zaccaria
● **End** 🚊 San Pietro

DAY TRIPS
Padua (1, C2)

A bustling medieval university town, Padua is also a glittering treasure chest of art. The nucleus of old Padua is formed by Piazza delle Erbe and Piazza della Frutta, colourful market squares separated by the majestic **Palazzo della Ragione** (€8/4; ☼9am-7pm Tue-Sun). The frescoed *salone* on the first floor is magnificent. Pilgrims flock to the **Basilica del Santo** (Basilica di Sant'Antonio; Piazza del Santo; ☼6.30am-7pm Nov-Feb, 6.30am-7.45pm Mar-Oct) to venerate the memory of Padua's patron saint, St Anthony, who is buried there. A different kind of pilgrimage has art lovers streaming in to behold the vision of Giotto's fresco cycle in the **Cappella degli Scrovegni** (☎049 201 00 20; www .cappelladegliscrovegni.it; Giardini dell'Arena; Tue-Sun €12/8, Mon

INFORMATION
37km west of Venice
- 🚆 Padua, up to 40 minutes
- 💶 PadovaCard (€14, valid 48 hours) for all main sights
- ℹ️ tourist office (☎049 876 79 27; www.turismopadova.it; Vicolo Pedrocchi & at the train station)
- 🍴 Per Bacco (☎049 875 46 64; Piazzale Pontecorvo 10)

Basilica of Padua's patron saint, Anthony

€8/5, booking required; ☼9am-7pm). Completed in 1306, the cycle presages the creative explosion of the Renaissance.

Riviera del Brenta (1, D2)

A riverboat ride past grand Venetian villas makes a charming one-day outing. Leaving from Riva degli Schiavoni in Venice, the boat meanders to the Brenta River, along which it proceeds to Strà, making stops at villas built by Venice's grandees as far back as the 16th century. First up is **Villa Foscari** (1571), a gem by Andrea Palladio, at **Malcontenta**. Next comes an early-18th-century rococo caprice west of **Oriago**, the **Villa Widmann Foscari**. Its most impressive elements are the ballroom (Sala delle Feste) and manicured garden. Further on, **Villa Pisani** is by far the grandest of the villas. It is set in extensive gardens just short of **Strà** and was completed in 1760 for Doge Alvise Pisani. In Strà itself is the imposing 17th-century **Villa Foscarini Rossi**.

INFORMATION
12-29km west of Venice
- 🚤 From Venice (Riva degli Schiavoni) Tue, Thu & Sat, then shuttle buses from Strà to Padua bus station
- ℹ️ Il Burchiello tour boat (☎049 820 69 10; www.ilburchiello.it; adult/child 12-18/child 6-12/child under 6 €62/44/31/free; operates Mar-Oct)
- 🍴 lunch included in excursion

Verona (1, A2)

Shakespeare thought the blood feuds of medieval Verona so intriguing he wrote a blockbusting play about them, *Romeo and Juliet*. The Veronese, in turn, were no slouches, and so 'little Rome' has for centuries also been sold to romantics as the city of the 'star-crossed lovers'. You can even see Juliet's house, the **Casa di Giulietta** (☎ 045 803 43 03; Via Cappello 23; adult/student/child €4/3/1; ۞ 8.30am-7.30pm Tue-Sun, 1.45-7.30pm Mon). Pity she didn't really exist!

A great deal more real is the 1st-century pink marble **Roman Arena** (☎ 045 800 32 04; www .arena.it; Piazza Brà; admission €4; ۞ 8.30am-6.30pm Tue-Sun, 1.30-6.30pm Mon, 8.30am-3.30pm during opera season), the third largest Roman amphitheatre in existence. It does a roaring trade as Verona's summer open-air opera house.

Originally the site of a Roman forum, **Piazza delle Erbe** remains the lively heart of the city today. Sumptuous buildings line the square, including the baroque **Palazzo Maffei** at the north end, with the adjoining 14th-century **Torre del Gardello**. On the east flank is the frescoed **Casa Mazzanti**, former residence of the medieval ruling della Scala clan. Ascend the nearby 12th-century **Torre dei Lamberti** (by elevator €3, on foot €2; ۞ 9am-7.30pm Tue-Sun, 1.30-7.30pm Mon) for the views.

The mantle of Verona is studded with the jewels of fine churches (combined ticket €5, admission to each €2). Seek out, in particular, the 12th-century **cathedral** (Piazza del Duomo; ۞ 10am-5.30pm Mon-Sat, 1.30-5.30pm Sun), which combines Romanesque (lower section) and Gothic (upper section) styles. Among the best of the rest are **Chiesa di Sant' Anastasia** (Piazza di Sant'Anastasia), **Chiesa di San Fermo** (Stradone San Fermo) and the **Basilica di San Zeno Maggiore** (Piazza San Zeno 2).

INFORMATION

120km west of Venice

🚉 Verona, 1¼-2¼ hours

ℹ️ tourist office (☎ 045 806 86 80; www.tourism.verona.it; Via degli Alpini 9)

✖️ Bottega del Vino (☎ 045 800 45 35; Vicolo Scudo di Francia 3/a)

Casa Mazzanti's allegorical frescoes

ORGANISED TOURS

Local travel agencies can put you onto city tours ranging from two-hour guided walks to gondola rides with a serenade for €35 per person. One such agency is **Agenzia Kele & Teo** (3, G4; ☎ 041 520 87 22; San Marco 4930).

Allegro in Venice

Join the 7.30am tour (for crowdless sightseeing), Running Venice (for jogging and sightseeing at once) or another tour chasing ghosts and legends. The Easy Access Venice service is aimed at helping the disabled enjoy the city.
☎ 041 528 77 78 🖳 www.allegroinvenice.com
€ tours €5-35

Basilica di San Marco Mosaics (3, H4)

The Patriarcato (church body in Venice) organises guided tours of the mosaics in St Mark's Basilica. You are given a detailed explanation of their biblical significance. The timetable can vary, so call ahead (10am-noon Mon-Fri) to be sure.
☎ 041 241 38 17 ✉ Piazza San Marco, San Marco
€ free ☼ English 11am Mon, Thu, Fri; French 11am Thu; Italian 11am Mon-Sat

Città d'Acqua (5, B1)

The Maree Veneziane tours explore various parts of the lagoon, including the Arsenale (otherwise virtually impossible to visit; p26), Malamocco (5, D4), Le Vignole (5, E2) and Giudecca (p34).
☎ 041 93 68 33 🖳 www.veniceitineraries.com
✉ Centro Internazionale Città d'Acqua, Officina Viaggi, Via Col Moschin 14, Mestre € per person up to €75 (minimum group of 40), per person up to €95 (group of 10-39)

RiViviNatura (3, E5)

This group organises offbeat day tours around the lagoon in anything from large traditional *bragozzi* under sail to a *vaporetto*. They are great for those who know Venice already and want to get a more unusual take on the city. RiViviNatura also does walking tours.
☎ 041 296 07 26
🖳 www.rivivinatura.it
✉ Calle dei Vitturi, San Marco 2923 € per person up to €50

Venice Events

This Italian-British outfit, apart from arranging

Paparazzi wait for the sun at Juliet's house, Verona

weddings and other events in Venice, puts on a series of tours. The Venice Past & Present tour from Piazza San Marco to the Rialto is the most regular and standard option.
☎ 041 523 99 79
🖳 www.veniceevents.com
✉ Frezzaria, San Marco 1827 € per person €20
☼ 11.15am Mon-Fri, 2pm Sat-Sun

Venicescapes

For luxury themed tours into the heart of Venetian history and mystery, this could be the tour group for you. Themes range from Story of a Mercantile Empire to the Age of Decadence.
🖳 www.venicescapes.org
€ US$150-250

Walks Inside Venice

A trio of ladies with a deep knowledge of Venice is behind this tour group. They will organise walks themed on anything from art to specific areas (such as Dorsoduro or Cannaregio) to *cicheti* (bar snacks) or craft workshops.
☎ 041 524 17 06
🖳 www.walksinsidevenice.com € typical 3hr tour €210

GENTLY DOWN THE STREAM

Eolo (☎ 049 807 80 32; www.cruisingvenice.com; Via Mantegna 11, 35020 Brugine PD) takes you aboard the like-named 1946 *bragozzo*, a heavy-hulled lagoon sailing vessel, for lagoon cruises of one to eight days. They involve tootling about the lagoon and sometimes up the Brenta River, with meals aboard or on the mainland. These tours are for six to 12 people. The cost ranges from €330 per person for one day to €5800 for eight days.

Shopping

Venice offers shoppers endless scope for maxing out credit cards. If classic Venetian items such as Murano glass, Burano lace, marbled paper and Carnevale masks don't do it for you, a host of other options, from high fashion to handicrafts, will surely entice.

Shopping Areas

The main shopping area for clothing, shoes and accessories is in the narrow streets between Piazza San Marco (3, H5) and Rialto (3, G2), particularly the Mercerie (aka Marzarie; 3, G3) and around Campo San Luca (3, G4). More upmarket shops are west of Piazza San Marco.

For Carnevale masks, costumes, delicatessen items, ceramics and crafts, San Polo (3) is the best hunting ground. Another Venetian speciality, marbled paper, is found all over town. Murano glass can be obtained on Murano (2, G1) or in shops mainly in the San Marco area (3). Lace, another speciality, is most easily bought on the island of Burano (5, F1), although several shops in Venice also sell it.

Opening Hours & Taxes

Store opening hours are about 9.30am to 7.30pm, with a two-hour break from 1pm or 1.30pm. Bigger stores and increasingly some small shops skip the lunch break. Most shops open on Saturday and some, anxious to attract every tourist euro, on Sunday too. Several shops shut through at least part of August.

Venini's top-shelf Murano glassware (p49)

If you are resident outside the EU, you are entitled to claim a VAT (IVA in Italy) refund on purchases where you spend more than €155 in one store.

INSIDER VIEW: MY SHOPPING FAVOURITES

Distracted by the architectural beauty that is frequently an inevitable feature of Venice's stores, it can be hard to concentrate on the serious business of shopping. To get focused, I wander the Mercatino dei Miracoli (Little Market of Miracles; p50), on Campo Santa Maria Nova or Via Garibaldi, held on the first weekend of each month and busy with all sorts of used, old and antique odds and sods. For fun and affordable costume jewellery I love to rummage at Perle e Dintorni (p50). And the two Venetian sisters at Godi Fiorenza (p49) make some wonderful threads!

Luisa De Salvo, Head of Public Relations, APT (Venice's tourism body)

ART

The single biggest concentration of galleries, selling a variety of art, is in the Dorsoduro area on the streets that lie between the Gallerie dell'Accademia (3, D6) and the Peggy Guggenheim Collection (3, E6), as well as along Calle del Bastion (3, F6). Calle delle Carrozze (3, D5) and the surrounding streets in San Marco are also worth a look.

BAC Art Studio (3, D6)
This studio has paintings, aquatints and engravings by Cadore and Paolo Baruffaldi, which can make fine gifts. Cadore concentrates his commercial efforts on street and canal scenes, while Baruffaldi mainly depicts masked people. There are also quality postcards.
☎ 041 522 81 71 ✉ Campo San Vio, Dorsoduro 862 ☽ 10am-1pm & 2-6.30pm Mon-Sat ⚓ Accademia

Galleria Ferruzzi (2, D5)
Ferruzzi's images of Venice are an engaging, almost naïve distortion of what we see. With fat brush strokes and primary colours, the artist creates a kind of children's gingerbread Venice.

You'll find screen prints, paintings and postcard versions.
☎ 041 522 85 82 ✉ Fondamenta Zorzi Bragadin, Dorsoduro 523 ☽ 10am-6.30pm Wed-Sat & Mon ⚓ Accademia

Galleria Traghetto (3, F5)
A stalwart on the Venetian art scene, this is one of the most respected of the few galleries dealing in contemporary artists, mostly Italian but open to international flavours.
☎ 041 522 11 88 ✉ Calle di Piovan, San Marco 2543 ☽ 3-7pm Mon-Sat ⚓ Santa Maria del Giglio

La Galleria van der Koelen (3, F5)
The Venice branch of this German gallery injects a contemporary flavour into the local scene, which apart from during the Biennale can be rather conservative. It frequently stages exhibitions of international artists, which are worth seeing whether you're a buyer or not.
☎ 041 520 74 15 ▢ www.galerie.vanderkoelen.de ✉ Ramo Primo dei Calegheri, San Marco 2566 ☽ 10am-1pm & 3.30-7pm Mon-Sat ⚓ Santa Maria del Giglio

ANTIQUES & CRAFTS

A Mano (3, D3)
Everything is handmade in this bric-a-brac shop. Quirky lampshades, mirrors and a host of other gewgaws certainly make it an interesting stop for a browse.
☎ 041 71 57 42 ✉ Rio Terà, San Polo 2616 ☽ 10am-1pm & 2.30-7.30pm Tue-Sat ⚓ San Tomà

Antiquus (3, E4)
Step back in time in this old-style store with the haphazard look. It boasts a collection of old masters, silverware and antique jewellery. Alongside the few items of furniture sit grand tea sets and other aristocratic bric-a-brac.
☎ 041 520 63 95 ✉ Calle delle Botteghe, San Marco 3131 ☽ 2.30-7pm Mon, 10am-1pm & 2.30-7pm Tue-Sun ⚓ San Samuele

Arca (3, D1)
For those with a love of strong statements in design and colour, the ceramics of Teresa della Valentina could be the go. She paints her tiles and a variety of other ceramic objects in bold, bright, deep hues.
☎ 041 71 04 27 ✉ Calle del Tintor, Santa Croce 1811 ☽ 9.30am-7pm ⚓ San Stae

Gilberto Penzo (3, D3)
Here you can buy exquisite hand-built wooden models of various Venetian vessels. Mr Penzo also takes in old ones for restoration. For the kids, snap up the gondola model kits.
☎ 041 71 93 72 ✉ Calle 2 dei Saoneri, San Polo 2681

Imaginings at BAC Art Studio

GILBERTO'S GONDOLAS

Gilberto Penzo long ago became passionate about gondolas. He began to build models and collect detailed plans of them and all sorts of other traditional lagoon and Adriatic vessels. Fearful that much of Venice's boatbuilding traditions will be lost, he founded an association to keep this ancient knowledge alive, and to finance it all opened his shop.

Gilberto Penzo's models of traditional Venetian vessels

☽ 9am-12.30pm & 3-6pm Mon-Sat ♨ San Tomà

Laboratorio del Gervasuti (2, F4)

A family business since the 1950s, this somewhat scruffy-looking workshop is jammed with all sorts of curious antiques, but if you are a serious purchaser ask to see the warehouse.

☎ 392 677 90 00 ✉ Campo Bandiera e Moro, Castello 3725 ☽ Fri-Sat, otherwise by appointment ♨ San Zaccaria

Le Forcole di Saverio Pastor (3, E6)

You can't find much more Venetian than a shop selling *forcole*. What on earth is a *forcola*? Well, it's the twisted wooden bit on which gondoliers rest their oars. You can buy the real thing for your gondola or baby ones as souvenirs.

☎ 041 522 56 99 ✉ Fondamenta Soranzo detta Fornace, Dorsoduro 341 ☽ 8.30am-12.30pm & 2.30-6pm Mon-Sat ♨ Salute

Livio de Marchi (3, D5)

Fancy a wooden sculpture of an unironed shirt? Or perhaps a pair of underpants? Local sculptor De Marchi has found a market for his strange and sometimes gigantic representations, mostly of everyday objects, from raincoats to bras. He also sculpts in glass.

☎ 041 528 56 94 💻 www.liviodemarchi.com ✉ Salizada San Samuele, San Marco 3157/a ☽ 9am-noon & 2-6pm Mon-Fri ♨ San Samuele

Martinuzzi (3, G5)

Pick up high-class doilies at one of the city's traditional purveyors of fine Burano lace. The little store is draped in luxurious lace and also festooned with Murano glass.

☎ 041 522 50 68 ✉ Piazza San Marco 67/a ☽ 9am-7.30pm Mon-Sat, 9am-7pm Sun ♨ Vallaresso & San Marco

Sabbie e Nebbie (3, D3)

The speciality in this ceramics boutique is tea time, with a range of hand-crafted tea and coffee pots and sets. You'll also find elegant Japanese imports, from tea sets to sushi platters.

☎ 041 71 90 73 ✉ Calle dei Nomboli, San Polo 2768/a ☽ 10am-12.30pm & 4-7.30pm ♨ San Tomà

Valese (3, H4)

Since 1918 the Valese family has been casting figures in bronze and other metals. Not all the items might suggest themselves as souvenirs, but the horses that adorn the flanks of the city's gondolas are tempting.

☎ 041 522 72 82 ✉ Calle Fiubera, San Marco 793 ☽ 10.30am-7pm Mon-Sat ♨ Vallaresso & San Marco

De Marchi's frozen moments

BOOKS & MUSIC

Editore Filippi (3, H4)
This is a den of books on all manner of subjects related to Venice, many published and sold exclusively here (much in Italian only). The Filippis have been in the business for nearly a century. Scholars search them out for their encyclopaedic knowledge. ☎ 041 523 56 35 ✉ Calle Casselleria, Castello 5763 ⏰ 9am-12.30pm & 3.30-7.30pm Mon-Sat 🚊 San Zaccaria

Librairie Française (2, F4)
Voulez-vous vos livres en français? Here you will find everything from the latest bestsellers of Gallic literature to a plethora of titles on all subjects Venetian – the lot of it in French. ☎ 041 522 96 59 ✉ Barbaria de le Tole, Castello 6358 ⏰ 9am-12.30pm & 3.30-7pm Mon-Sat 🚊 Ospedale Civile

Libreria Linea d'Acqua (3, F4)
This small but useful shop offers a solid range of guides and other books on Venice, as well as children's books, many in English and some in

Vivaldi Store – be serenaded by Venice's darling

French. The shop also stocks Donna Leon's mystery detective yarns and specialises in antique books on Venice. ☎ 041 522 40 30 🖥 www.lineadacqua.it ✉ Calle della Cortesia, San Marco 3717/d ⏰ 10.30am-12.30pm & 4-6.45pm Mon-Sat 🚊 Rialto

Vivaldi Store (3, G3)
Looking for a Vivaldi or Albinoni CD? This is your place. Cristiano Nalesso specialises in all things musically Venetian, from the Renaissance through to baroque. ☎ 041 522 13 43 ✉ Salizada del Fontego dei Tedeschi, San Marco 5537 ⏰ 9.30am-7pm Mon-Sat, 11am-7pm Sun 🚊 Rialto

CARNEVALE MASKS & COSTUMES

Atelier Pietro Longhi (3, D3)
Ever fancied a helmet and sword to go with your tailor-made Carnevale costume? Maybe a Harlequin outfit, or just a top hat? This is one of the classic costume stores. ☎ 041 71 44 78 ✉ Rio Terà, San Polo 2604/b ⏰ 10am-noon & 3-7pm Mon-Fri, 10am-noon Sat 🚊 San Tomà

Ca' Macana (3, C5)
Wander in and watch the artists at work on the raw papier-mâché of future masks in this, one of the better mask-makers in the city. Business is booming and they have a couple of other stores around town. ☎ 041 277 61 42 🖥 www.camacana.com ✉ Calle delle Botteghe, Dorsoduro 3172 ⏰ 10am-6.30pm 🚊 Ca' Rezzonico

L'Arlecchino (3, F2)
Here they claim the masks are made only with papier-mâché

VENICE READS
- *Death in Venice* – Thomas Mann
- *Night Letters* – Robert Dessaix
- *The Comfort of Strangers* – Ian McEwan
- *A History of Venice* – John Julius Norwich
- *Venice: The Biography of a City* – Christopher Hibbert
- *The Merchant of Venice* – William Shakespeare
- *The Venetian Empire, A Sea Voyage* – Jan Morris
- *A Venetian Reckoning* – Donna Leon
- *Miss Garnet's Angel* – Sally Vickers

Does the mask conceal or reveal? Find out at Ca' Macana (p47)

to their own designs. You can often see people making masks here and in any case the quality is evident.

☎ 041 520 82 20 ✉ Ruga del Ravano, San Polo 789 ☾ 9.30am-7.30pm Mon-Sat ⛟ San Silvestro

Mondonovo Maschere (3, B5)

Like many other shops in Venice, this workshop and boutique doesn't seem much from the outside, but one of the city's master mask-makers, Guerrino Lovato, is behind it all. He was commissioned to provide some of the masks for Stanley Kubrick's *Eyes Wide Shut*.

☎ 041 528 73 44 ▢ www .mondonovomaschere.it ✉ Rio Terà Canal, Dorsoduro 3063 ☾ 9am-6pm Mon-Sat ⛟ Ca' Rezzonico

Tragicomica (3, D3)

One of the bigger mask and costume merchants, Tragicomica also organises costume parties during Carnevale. The place is quite overwhelming at first sight.

☎ 041 72 11 02 ▢ www .tragicomica.it ✉ Calle Nomboli, San Polo 2800 ☾ 10am-1.30pm & 2.30-7pm ⛟ San Tomà

FOOD & DRINK

Aliani (3, F2)

For an outstanding assortment of cheeses and other delicatessen products, Aliani has long been a favoured stop in the Rialto. You will also find a range of wines and other products.

☎ 041 522 49 13 ✉ Ruga Vecchia di San Giovanni, San Polo 654 ☾ 8am-1pm & 5-7.30pm Tue-Sat ⛟ Rialto

Caffè Costarica (4, C2)

Since 1930 the Marchi family has been importing coffee from Costa Rica and other coffee-producing countries, and toasting it daily for your delectation. You can also try some at the bar.

Indulge at Drogheria Mascari

☎ 041 71 63 71 ✉ Rio Terà San Leonardo, Cannaregio 1337 ☾ 8am-1pm & 3.30-7.30pm Mon-Sat ⛟ San Marcuola

Drogheria Mascari (3, F2)

The Drogheria Mascari is another Venetian foodies' classic. Jars of goods, salty and sweet, are accompanied by a mouth-watering range of sweets, including slabs of chocolate and nougat.

☎ 041 522 97 62 ✉ Ruga degli Spezieri, San Polo 381 ☾ 8am-1pm & 4-7.30pm Thu-Tue, 8am-1pm Wed ⛟ Rialto

GLASS & CRYSTAL

Berengo (2, G1)

Here is a purveyor of glass that has long abandoned any pretence at functionality in its products. This is glass for art's sake. If you are into the idea of glass as sculpture, this is an interesting stop.

☎ 041 527 63 64 ▢ www .berengo.com ✉ Fondamenta dei Vetrai 109/a, Murano ☾ 10am-6pm ⛟ Colonna

L'Isola (3, G5)

Carlo Moretti designs a range of functional and decorative glass items, often boasting deep primary colours and always oozing elegance.

☎ 041 523 19 73 ▢ www .carlomoretti.com ✉ Campo San Moisè, San Marco 1468 ☾ 9am-7pm ⛟ Vallaresso & San Marco

Marco Polo (2, G1)

Marco Polo offers you the opportunity to see the masters at work amid a vast display of traditional

THE TOSO BORELLA TOUCH

The glass-making clans of Murano have centuries of history. Francesco Toso Borella came to fame in the late 19th century for fine decorative gold and enamel etchings done on Murano glass objects. His son Vittorio followed suit, especially with Art Nouveau designs. Their descendent, Marco (b 1962), is acclaimed as a veritable artist in glass. Applying his first love, painting, to glasswork, some of his best works have been the transformation of great paintings, such as Leonardo da Vinci's *Last Supper*, into shimmering golden glass replicas.

glassware; you can also have objects tailor-made and sent to your country. Upstairs is a museum of contemporary glass, with names from local master Andrea Pagnes to international creators.
☎ 041 73 99 04 🖳 www .marcopologlass.it ✉ Fondamenta Manin 1, Murano ⏰ 9am-5pm 🚢 Colonna

Venini (2, G1)

Venini is another top-shelf name in artistic glassware and crystal. It also has a **branch** (3, H4; ☎ 041 522 40 45; Piazzetta dei Leoni, San Marco 314) in central Venice.
☎ 041 273 99 55 🖳 www .venini.it ✉ Fondamenta dei Vetrai 47-50, Murano ⏰ 9am-5.30pm Mon-Sat 🚢 Colonna

CLOTHING, SHOES & ACCESSORIES

Antica Modisteria Giuliana Longo (3, G3)

If hats ever come back, this place will be well placed to ride the new wave. From gondoliers' caps to extravagant ladies' millinery, this is the place to scratch around for all sorts of headgear.
☎ 041 522 64 54 ✉ Calle del Lovo, San Marco 4813

⏰ 10am-7pm Mon-Sat 🚢 Rialto

Attombri (3, G3)

Along a gallery once lined by prosperous goldsmiths, this is one of the few jewellers doing well on this stretch. The inventive, 'Byzantine'-style jewellery constitutes a captivating and original collection, and not just in gold.
☎ 041 521 25 24 🖳 www .attombri.com ✉ Sotoportego Oresi, San Polo 74 ⏰ 10am-1pm & 4-7pm Mon-Sat 🚢 Rialto

Codognato (3, G5)

The city's most emblematic jewellery shop opened for business in 1866, just as the Austrians were leaving and Venice was joining a newly united Italy. Ever since it has been the obligatory,

backstreet jewellery stop for anyone who is anyone.
☎ 041 522 50 42 ✉ Calle Seconda dell'Ascensione, San Marco 1295 ⏰ 4-7pm Mon, 10am-1pm & 4-7pm Tue-Sun Sep-Jun 🚢 Vallaresso & San Marco

Fanny (3, D3)

To avoid getting caught without the right stuff on your hands in winter, this spot has plenty of glove options, with some slinky models for her and classic cashmere-lined leather jobs for him.
☎ 041 522 82 66 ✉ Calle dei Saoneri, San Polo 2723 ⏰ 10am-7.30pm 🚢 San Tomà

Fiorella Gallery (3, E5)

You'll find all sorts of odd billowing and fantastical clothing items here. They adorn striking transsexual *doge* (duke) mannequins scattered about the inside and windows.
☎ 041 520 92 28 ✉ Campo Santo Stefano, San Marco 2806 ⏰ 10.30am-1pm & 3-7pm Mon-Sat 🚢 Accademia

Godi Fiorenza (3, G4)

Although their hearts are in London, the two Venetian sisters in charge here create a very personal line in fashion,

Gainfully employed 21st-century *doges* (dukes) at Fiorella

CLOTHING & SHOE SIZES

Women's Clothing

Aust/UK	8	10	12	14	16	18
Europe	36	38	40	42	44	46
Japan	5	7	9	11	13	15
USA	6	8	10	12	14	16

Women's Shoes

Aust/USA	5	6	7	8	9	10
Europe	35	36	37	38	39	40
France only	35	36	38	39	40	42
Japan	22	23	24	25	26	27
UK	3½	4½	5½	6½	7½	8½

Measurements approximate only; try before you buy.

Men's Clothing

Aust	92	96	100	104	108	112
Europe	46	48	50	52	54	56
Japan	S	M	M		L	
UK/USA	35	36	37	38	39	40

Men's Shirts (Collar Sizes)

Aust/Japan	38	39	40	41	42	43
Europe	38	39	40	41	42	43
UK/USA	15	15½	16	16½	17	17½

Men's Shoes

Aust/UK	7	8	9	10	11	12
Europe	41	42	43	44½	46	47
Japan	26	27	27.5	28	29	30
USA	7½	8½	9½	10½	11½	12½

hovering between the traditional and a carefully styled contemporary look.
☎ 041 241 08 66 ✉ Campo San Luca, San Marco 4261 ⏰ 10am-12.30pm & 3.30-7.30pm Mon-Sat 🚤 Rialto

Mazzon Le Borse (3, D3)
An unassuming workshop well known to Venetian shoppers, Mazzon produces handmade leather bags and accessories. The goods are top class and often better than many of the big names.
☎ 041 520 34 21 ✉ Campiello San Tomà, San Polo 2807 ⏰ 9am-12.30pm & 3.30-7.30pm Mon-Sat 🚤 San Tomà

Perle e Dintorni (3, F4)
You can have necklaces and other cheerful costume jewellery made to measure or simply pick and choose from the vast assortment of light and playful stuff on show here.
☎ 041 520 50 68 ✉ Calle della Mandola, San Marco 3740 ⏰ 9.30am-1pm & 2-7.30pm Mon-Sat, 2-7.30pm Sun 🚤 Rialto

Ronaldo Segalin (3, G4)
They don't make shoes like this any more. Well, except in places like this! Segalin produces classic men's footwear by hand, along with ladies' shoes and Carnevale-style 18th-century dress options.
☎ 041 522 21 15 ✉ Calle dei Fuseri, San Marco 4365 ⏰ 10am-12.30pm & 3.30-7pm 🚤 Rialto

MARKETS

Mercatino dei Miracoli (3, H2)
This is a bric-a-brac market that is held monthly in two alternating locations (for Via Garibaldi see 2, G5). You can turn up all sorts of things, from bric-a-brac to antiques, and the atmosphere is always fun.
✉ Campo Santa Maria Nova or Via Garibaldi ⏰ 1st weekend every month 🚤 Ca' d'Oro

Pescaria (3, F2)
Underneath the neo-Gothic roof built at the beginning of the 20th century, the Pescaria (Fish Market) gets a mixed clientele of domestic shoppers and restaurateurs in search of ingredients for the day's menu. They have been selling fish here for 700 years.
✉ Pescaria, Rialto, San Polo ⏰ 7am-2pm 🚤 traghetto from Campo Santa Sofia or vaporetto Rialto

Why they love their fruit and veg in the land of Slow Food

Rialto Produce Markets (3, G2)

The raucous cries of vendors rise above the general hubbub as the canny shoppers of Venice rub shoulders with unsuspecting neophyte tourists. A local favourite is the humble artichoke, prized by Venetians. Buy yourself the makings of a picnic.

✉ Rialto, San Polo ⏰ 7am-2pm 🚏 Rialto or traghetto from Campo Santa Sofia

PAPER & STATIONERY

Venice is noted for its *carta marmorizzata* (marbled paper), used for all sorts of things, from expensive gift wrap to book covers.

Il Papiro (3, E5)

A bright, spacious stationer, Il Papiro doesn't pretend to compete with the traditional paper shops. Among a fairly modest selection you will also find a range of more upscale items, such as elegant envelopes and letter openers.

☎ 041 522 30 55 ✉ Calle del Spezier, San Marco 2764 ⏰ 10.30am-7pm 🚏 Santa Maria del Giglio

Il Pavone (3, E6)

The dominant colours (blues, reds and yellows) and motifs (floral shapes, cherubs and others) at Il Pavone change from one day to the next. The templates are applied equally to hand-printed paper as well as to ties and other objects. You can have T-shirts made here, too.

☎ 041 523 45 17 ✉ Fondamenta Venier dai Leoni,

Dorsoduro 721 ⏰ 9.30am-1.30pm & 2.30-6.30pm 🚏 Accademia

Legatoria Polliero (3, D3)

A traditional exponent of the art of Venetian bookbinding with (and without) marbled paper. You barely have room to stand in this den, with stacks of leather-bound books, paper-bound folders and all sorts of other stationery piled higgledy-piggledy high to the rafters.

☎ 041 528 51 30 ✉ Campo dei Frari, San Polo 2995 ⏰ 10am-1.30pm & 3.30-7.30pm Mon-Sat, 10am-1.30pm Sun 🚏 San Tomà

FOR CHILDREN

Disney Store (3, G3)

Like it or not, kids love Disney toys and this place may well save a failing parental relationship with little ones at a key moment during your Venetian wanders. It's called bribery.

☎ 041 522 39 80 ✉ Campo San Bartolomeo, San Marco 5257 ⏰ 9.30am-7.30pm 🚏 Rialto

Gilberto Penzo (3, D3)

See p45.

Il Baule Blu (3, D4)

Those who remember childhood without Playstation could swing by to admire the teddy bears, dolls and ancient toys of another era. Perhaps you'll strike an atavistic chord in your 21st-century offspring too!

☎ 041 71 94 48 ✉ Campo San Tomà, San Polo 2916/a ⏰ 10.30am-12.30pm & 4-7.30pm Mon-Sat 🚏 San Tomà

Legno e Dintorni (3, C5)

Original souvenirs that children might like to take home are the wooden models of Venetian monuments and façades, akin to simple 3-D puzzles.

☎ 041 522 63 67 ✉ Fondamenta Gherardini, Dorsoduro 2840 ⏰ 10am-1.30pm & 2-7pm 🚏 Ca' Rezzonico

Molin Giocattoli (3, G2)

Sitting by what locals call Toys Bridge (Ponte dei Giocattoli), this shop will attract kids with a yen for things like a model Ferrari or *vaporetto*.

☎ 041 523 52 85 ✉ Salizada San Canciano, Cannaregio 5899 ⏰ 10.30am-12.30pm & 4-7.30pm Mon-Fri, 4-7.30pm Sat 🚏 Rialto

Like bees to honey: checking out Molin Giocattoli's display

Eating

Can one eat well in Venice? Ask an Italian and you may be greeted by a contemptuous snort. Dining is more expensive than elsewhere in Italy, and palming off second-rate food to unwitting tourists is a Venetian sport.

But plenty of places, from the modest *osteria* (traditional bar/restaurant) to the impeccable luxury of Harry's Bar (opposite), constitute healthy exceptions. After all, they have the locals to satisfy too!

Among the most promising areas are San Polo and Santa Croce between the Rialto and Campo San Giacomo dell'Orio (3). In Dorsoduro, you'll discover all sorts of goodies around Campo Santa Margherita (3, B4). Several interesting spots hover around where the districts of San Marco, Cannaregio and Castello meet.

A full meal consists of an *antipasto* (starter), a *primo piatto* (second course) – usually pasta, risotto or soup – and a *secondo* (second course) of fish or meat. Venice is a seaside town and fish predominates. Meals finish with a *dolce* (dessert) and *caffè*. You can often eat more cheaply at lunch if you opt for a set menu. Most cuisine is local or more broadly Italian. Venetians in the mood for foreign fare have a hard time. Aside from a few bog standard Chinese places, the odd kebab stand and McDonald's, there is only a handful of interesting alternatives (including Japanese and Indian).

> **IL CONTO (THE BILL)**
> The price ranges used here indicate the cost per person of a two-course meal, including a bottle of modest wine:
>
> | € | €25 and under |
> |---|---|
> | €€ | €26-40 |
> | €€€ | €41-80 |
> | €€€€ | over €80 |

Restaurants generally open for lunch (12.30pm to 3pm) but often stop taking orders after 2pm. Evening dining starts at 7.30pm with few places serving after 10.30pm. Unless noted otherwise, all places reviewed in this chapter are open for lunch and dinner.

> **SIDE-STEPPING BAD SALAD**
> Steer clear of restaurants along tourist thoroughfares (such as the Lista di Spagna; 4, B3) advertising impossibly cheap three-course menus. Touts and multilingual menus are also a sign you could be treated to sloppy, microwaved impersonations of food. Watch out for the tour groups scoffing tired salad and droopy pasta.

For *cicheti* (bar snacks) and local wine Venetians traditionally seek out a *bacaro* or *osteria*. The latter can also be an inn offering a limited menu of simple food and house wines. A *trattoria* is traditionally a simpler, family-run version of a *ristorante*, although such distinctions are often blurred nowadays.

Smoking is banned in pretty much all restaurants, unless they have a specially separate and ventilated section for smokers.

SAN MARCO

Caffè Florian (3, H5)
Café €€

The plush interior of this, the city's best-known café, has seen the likes of Lord Byron and Henry James taking breakfast (separately) before they crossed the piazza to Caffè Quadri for lunch. In 1720 Venetians started paying exorbitant sums for the pleasure of drinking here. To pay less, drink at the bar.

☎ 041 520 56 41 ✉ Piazza San Marco 56-59 ⏰ 10am-midnight Thu-Tue 🚤 Vallaresso & San Marco

Caffé Florian: breakfast haunt of Lord Byron and Henry James

Caffè Quadri (3, H4)
Café & Restaurant €€

Quadri is in much the same league as Florian, and equally steeped in history. Indeed, it opened its doors before its better known competitor, in 1683. It also has a renowned restaurant upstairs. On the square, a quartet competes with those of Florian and other bars (watch the surcharge).

☎ 041 522 21 05 ✉ Piazza San Marco 120 ⏰ 9am-11.30pm 🚤 Vallaresso & San Marco

Enoteca Il Volto (3, F3)
Wine Bar €€

Near Campo San Luca, this spot has an excellent wine selection and a tempting array of snacks, which will no doubt induce you to hang about for more than one glass. It is a classic of the Venetian scene.

☎ 041 522 89 45 ✉ Calle Cavalli 4081 ⏰ Mon-Sat 🚤 Rialto

Harry's Bar (3, G5)
Restaurant/Bar €€€€

The Cipriani family, who started this bar in 1931, claims to have invented many Venetian specialities, including the Bellini cocktail. On the culinary side, they also claim the patent for *carpaccio* (very fine slices of raw meat). Toscanini, Chaplin, Hemingway and just about everyone who was anyone (and quite a few who were definitely no-one) have eaten (and drunk) here.

☎ 041 528 57 77 ✉ Calle Vallaresso 1323 ⏰ daily 🚤 Vallaresso & San Marco

Lavena (3, H4)
Café €

Founded in 1750 and less celebrated than its big brothers (Florian and Quadri), Lavena is in the same vein. Wagner was among its more visible customers, but historically gondoliers and *codegas* (stout fellows who lit the way home for people returning at night) also hung out here.

☎ 041 522 40 70 ✉ Piazza San Marco 133 ⏰ 9.30am-12.30am Apr-Oct, 9am-10pm Wed-Mon Nov-Mar 🚤 Vallaresso & San Marco

Osteria alla Botte (3, G3)
Osteria €€

This youthful backstreet *bacaro* (much the same thing as an *osteria*) near the Rialto bridge is ideal for *cicheti* and a glass or two of *prosecco* (sparkling wine) at the bar. You could also opt for simple

Label gazing is a Venetian sport at Enoteca Il Volto

Try strawberry-flavoured *fragolino* wine at Osteria alla Botte

sit-down meals. Finish off with a glass of strawberry-flavoured *fragolino* wine.
☎ 041 520 97 75 ✉ Calle della Bissa 5482 🕑 Mon-Wed, Fri & Sat, lunch Sun 🚊 Rialto

Vini da Arturo (3, F4)
Meat €€€€
Welcome to carnivore heaven. This is one of those rare items in Venice, a restaurant that seems to have all but banned the presence of creatures from the deep. Sizzling slabs of meat are accompanied by respectable vegetable garnishes.
☎ 041 528 69 74 ✉ Calle dei Assassini 3656 🕑 Mon-Sat 🚊 Sant Angelo

Vino Vino (3, F5)
Venetian €
This fine old wine bar (it claims to offer 350 labels) can also be heartily recommended as a comfortable, economical eatery. A limited menu might include classics such as *sarde in saor* (large sardines in an onion and pine-nut dressing), but that depends on the day. Or you can accompany your tipple with bar snacks.
☎ 041 241 76 88 ✉ Calle della Veste 2007/a 🕑 Wed-

Mon 🚊 Santa Maria del Giglio

DORSODURO

Ai Gondolieri (2, D5)
Meat €€€€
Ai Gondolieri is another fabulous stop for meat-lovers. All mains are land-going critters (such as Angus steak, duck and liver). Dishes can be accompanied by a select offering of wine.
☎ 041 528 63 96 ✉ Fondamenta Ospedaleto 366 🕑 daily 🚊 Accademia

Enoteca Ai Artisti (3, C5)
Italian €
With a handful of tables outside and a glassed-in shopfront, this is a cheerful stop for a glass of good wine and a light meal, which could

range from *bruschetta* (Tuscan-style toast with topping) through to various *insalatoni* (big salads) to various pasta dishes and mains.
☎ 041 523 89 44 🖳 www .enotecaartisti.com ✉ Fondamenta de la Toletta 1169/a 🕑 Mon-Sat 🚊 Accademia

Fujiyama Beatrice Teahouse (3, B5)
Teahouse €
This vaguely eccentric tea-house along a busy gourmet street has a courtyard out the back and rents out a few charming little rooms upstairs. It's a pleasant spot to take the weight off during the day's sightseeing (tea and cake €4).
☎ 041 724 10 42 ✉ Calle Lunga San Barnaba 2727/a 🕑 1-8pm Mon-Fri 🚊 Ca' Rezzonico 🚻

Linea d'Ombra (2, E5)
Seafood €€€
Slightly overpriced, but the quality of the seafood in this designer restaurant is undeniable. On balmy nights and sunny days, try to grab a table on the pontoon, with wonderful views out the Bacino di San Marco. If the city's mayor likes it, they must be doing something right!

Ristorante La Bitta: keeping the carnivores happy

☎ 041 241 18 81 ✉ Ponte dell'Umiltà 19 ⊗ Thu-Tue 🚊 Salute

Osteria ai Quatro Feri
(3, C5)
Seafood €€
Seafood is the deal here. Tuna is a house speciality but you can also tuck into some swordfish at your cosy oak table. The *antipasti* are a possible option in place of pasta first courses, with a good mixed grill of vegetables or seafood salad, with plenty of octopus and other tempting sea critters.
☎ 041 520 69 78 ✉ Calle Lunga San Barnaba 2754/b ⊗ Mon-Sat 🚊 Ca' Rezzonico

Osteria da Toni (3, A6)
Venetian €€
For simple workaday lunches, this is a knockabout noshery where you'll get no-nonsense grub. Sit at one of the handful of tables outside or fight your way inside for a cramped table out the back. It's a house-wine sloshing, bang the plates down on the table kind of place.
☎ 041 523 82 72 ✉ Fondamenta San Basegio 1642 ⊗ Tue-Sun 🚊 San Basilio ♿

Osteria San Pantalon
(3, C3)
Venetian €€
Students with an eye for good local grub crowd in here for non-fussy Venetian fare, including *baccalà mantecato* (mashed-up cod prepared in garlic and parsley) and *sarde in saor*.
☎ 041 71 08 49 ✉ Calle del Scaleter 3958 ⊗ Mon-Fri & dinner Sat 🚊 San Tomà

Ristorante La Bitta
(3, C5)
Meat €€
The short menu is dominated by meat dishes, with veal, Angus steaks and similar carnivorous options in the lead. The bottle-lined dining room leads to an attractive internal courtyard. At the bar you'll find a few *cicheti* too.
☎ 041 523 05 31 ✉ Calle Lunga San Barnaba 2753/a ⊗ dinner Tue-Sat 🚊 Ca' Rezzonico

Ristorante Riviera (3, B6)
Italian €€€
Candlelit dining on balmy Venetian nights on the *fondamenta* (canalside footpath) is one of the key calling cards of this spot. The menu, an even balancing act between fish and meat at the main-course level, leaves the way open to most tastes, and includes a few Venetian specialities.
☎ 041 522 76 21 ✉ Fondamenta delle Zattere 1473 ⊗ Tue-Sun 🚊 San Basilio

SAN POLO

All'Arco (3, F2)
Osteria €€
For good-value *cicheti* and a glass of wine or two, this is one of the most authentic *osterie* in the San Polo area. People gather around the bar

Gather around the bar or pull up a stool at All' Arco

or, on warmer days, huddle together on stools by little tables in among the hubbub of the cramped lanes near the Rialto.
☎ 041 520 56 66 ✉ Calle dell'Arco 436 ⊗ 7am-5pm Mon-Sat 🚊 San Silvestro

Antiche Carampane
(3, E2)
Venetian €€€
If you manage to navigate to this place in the heart of the one-time red light district (nearby is Ponte delle Tette, or Tits Bridge), you will be in for good home-cooked fresh fish and vegetables with no concessions to cheap tourist menus.
☎ 041 524 01 65 ✉ Rio Terà delle Carampane 1911 ⊗ Tue-Sat 🚊 San Stae

Banco Giro (3, G2)
Italian €€
Long a simple market bar, this place is now at the heart of the convivial atmosphere (especially in the warmer months) around Rialto. Take a seat by the Grand Canal for a broad range of local and Italian cooking, albeit limited by the tiny kitchen's capacity, and drinkies. In winter, crowd into the bite-size bar.
☎ 041 523 20 61 ✉ Campo San Giacomo di Rialto 122 ⊗ Tue-Sun 🚊 Rialto

FOOD WITH A VIEW

- Harry's Dolci (p61)
- Linea d'Ombra (p54)
- Mistrà (p61)
- Naranzaria (right)
- Ristorante Riviera (p55)

Naranzaria: where East meets West, canalside

Bucintoro (3, D2)

Pastry shop €

Gino Zanin carries on antique Venetian traditions with his sweets and pastries, which come with such wonderful names as *bacingondola* (kiss in the gondola), which is a little meringue and chocolate number.

☎ 041 72 15 03 ✉ Calle del Scaleter 2229 ⏱ 7.15am-8pm Tue-Sun 🚊 San Stae

Cantina Do Mori (3, F2)

Osteria €€

Hidden away near the Ponte di Rialto, this is something of a traditional institution. It oozes history and attracts a lot of local custom for such items as its *francobolli* (stamps), tiny little sandwich snacks, and *cicheti,* washed down with an *ombra* (glass) of house white or *prosecco.*

☎ 041 522 54 01 ✉ Sotoportego dei do Mori 429 ⏱ 8.30am-8.30pm Mon-Sat 🚊 Rialto

Frary's (3, D3)

Middle Eastern €

A vague whiff of Middle Eastern chill and a broad menu encompassing Turkish dolmades, a couple of Greek dishes (moussaka €11), North African couscous and Arab faves like falafel make this a great change from Italian fare at very reasonable prices.

☎ 041 72 00 50 ✉ Fondamenta dei Frari 2559 ⏱ Wed-Mon 🚊 San Tomà Ⓥ

Ganesh Ji (3, C2)

Indian €€

Fancy a quick curry? Forget it. But a good slow one can be had on the pleasant little canalside terrace of this place. Staff serve up authentic dishes at reasonable prices – pleased guests have scribbled their appreciation on the walls. Try the vegetarian set meal (€14.50) or the meaty equivalent (€16).

☎ 041 71 90 84 ✉ Fondamenta Rio Marin 2426 ⏱ Fri-Tue, dinner Wed-Thu 🚊 Ferrovia Ⓥ

Muro Vino e Cucina (3, G2)

Italian €€€

Upstairs from the designer-bar scene take a seat in a gleaming industrial-style setting. Try for a seat by the grand windows overlooking the market area. There is nothing overly Venetian about what's on offer, which can range from steak Châteaubriand to grilled fish of the day.

☎ 041 523 47 40 ✉ Campo Cesare Battisti 222 ⏱ Mon-Sat 🚊 Rialto

Naranzaria (3, G2)

Fusion €€€

Venice meets Tokyo amid the Rialto markets for a fusion session of sushi and *cicheti,* along with light summer dishes (sit by the Grand Canal) and some fine local and Friuli wines. Another option is a table upstairs.

☎ 041 724 10 35 ✉ Campo San Giacomo di Rialto 130 ⏱ Tue-Sun 🚊 Rialto

SANTA CROCE

Ae Oche (3, D2)
Pizzeria €
Students love this place, with its low timber ceiling and old-style travel ads from the US on the walls. Choose from around 90 types of pizza and a good range of salads in a busy, youthful atmosphere. ☎ 041 524 11 61 ✉ Calle del Tintor 1552/a ⏰ daily 🚤 San Stae ♿

Al Nono Risorto (3, E2)
Pizzeria/Restaurant €€
We'd recommend you stop in here if only to luxuriate in the leafy canalside garden in summertime. In the cooler months customers head inside the lofty timber dining area. The pizzas (€5 to €9) in particular are good. Otherwise you could opt for a reasonable set-price lunch menu (€15). The service is friendly if a little scatty. ☎ 041 524 11 69 ✉ Sotoportego de Siora Bettina 2338 ⏰ Thu-Tue 🚤 San Stae ♿

Alaska (Da Pistacchi) (3, C1)
Gelateria €
The *gelati* here have something of the mythical about them. The flavours are as real as the colours are vibrant. Opening times can be erratic; we have seen Alaska serving ice cream around midnight, yet shut in the morning. ☎ 041 71 52 11 ✉ Calle Larga dei Bari 1159 ⏰ 8am-1pm & 3-8pm 🚤 Riva de Biasio

All'Anfora (3, C1)
Pizzeria €
Head out the back into the courtyard to indulge in an enormous choice of generous, tasty pizzas over a beer. You can opt for set lunches or meals *alla carta* too, but pizza is king.

☎ 041 524 03 25 ✉ Lista dei Bari 1223 ⏰ Thu-Tue 🚤 Riva de Biasio ♿

Il Refolo (3, D1)
Pizzeria/Restaurant €€
This place behind the Chiesa di San Giacomo dell'Orio on a quiet back canal is a local favourite for above-average pizza. It does a limited selection of pasta and main courses, salads and some melt-in-the-mouth desserts. ☎ 041 524 00 16 ✉ Campo San Giacomo dell'Orio 1459 ⏰ Wed-Sun, dinner Tue 🚤 Riva de Biasio ♿

Osteria La Zucca (3, D1)
Mediterranean €€
It seems like just another Venetian *trattoria*, but the menu (which changes daily) is an enticing mix of Mediterranean themes. The vegetable side orders (around €4.50) alone are inspired (try the *carotte al curry e yoghurt*, a carrot curry job), while the mains (€14 to €16) are substantial. You won't need to order pasta as well.

Osteria La Zucca: you'll think you're in the Mediterranean

Anice Stellato: warm, chatty and convivial

☎ 041 524 15 70 ⊠ Calle del Tintor 1762 ⏱ Mon-Sat ⚓ San Stae Ⓥ

Vecio Fritolin (3, E2)
Restaurant €€€
A *fritolin* was traditionally a kind of fish-and-polenta takeaway. Here they have revived the tradition at lunchtime. Better is to come for a classy evening meal, with a meticulous menu serving local and national dishes, home-baked bread and devilish desserts, all done with ingredients exclusively picked at the local Rialto markets.
☎ 041 522 28 81 ⊠ Calle della Regina 226 ⏱ Tue-Sun ⚓ San Stae Ⓥ

CANNAREGIO

Ai 40 Ladroni (4, D1)
Venetian & Pizza €€
In this den of the '40 Thieves' (without Ali Baba) you can feast on reasonable pizza or a range of typical Venetian seafood dishes, such as the Friday special, *baccalà mantecato*.
☎ 041 71 57 36 ⊠ Fondamenta della Sensa 3253 ⏱ Tue-Sun ⚓ Madonna dell'Orto

Anice Stellato (4, C1)
Trattoria €€€
Awaiting you in the guise of a doorman is a huge *damigiana* (demijohn). Inside, the heavy timber tables and chairs are perfect for a chatty, convivial meal. The pasta is excellent and the mains imaginative, including the occasional use of curry and other spices not immediately associated with either local or national cuisine.
☎ 041 72 07 44 ⊠ Fondamenta della Sensa 3272 ⏱ Wed-Sun ⚓ Madonna dell'Orto ♿

Boccadoro (3, H1)
Seafood €€€
Take a seat beneath the pleasant pergola on this quiet square for the freshest of seafood. The house special is the *fritto misto,* a delicate fry-up of fish, seafood and vegetables. If you want, the owner will explain the various merits of his fresh fish brought in from Chioggia that day.
☎ 041 521 10 21 ⊠ Campiello Widman 5405/a ⏱ Tue-Sun ⚓ Fondamente Nuove

Da Marisa (2, C2)
Trattoria €€
Expect robust meat-based cooking (Da Marisa is near the former abattoir but seems to have taken no notice of its demise). Options are rattled out loud and briskly – take a chance! You might get *petto d'anatra* (duck breast) or *fagiano ripieno* (stuffed pheasant).
☎ 041 72 02 11 ⊠ Fondamenta di San Giobbe 652/b ⏱ Tue & Thu-Sat, lunch Mon, Wed & Sun ⚓ Tre Archi

Enoteca alla Colombina (4, C2)
Tuscan & Venetian €€€
Just off the square, this delightful little spot offers some excellent versions of Tuscan cooking, including such classics as *tagliata di chianina* (succulent slices

SLY GROG SHOPS

Want some no-nonsense plonk for a picnic? Do what the locals do and take an empty mineral-water bottle to a wine store for about €2 per litre! Here are a few of Nave de Oro's several branches:

- Rio Terà San Leonardo, Cannaregio 1370 (4, C2)
- Calle dei SS Apostoli, Cannaregio 4657 (3, H1)
- Campo Santa Margherita, Dorsoduro 3664 (3, B4)
- Calle Mondo Nuovo, Castello 5786/b (3, H3)

of Tuscan beef) and *pan-zanella*, a tasty gathering of 'leftovers', including tomato, bread and onion, in a crunchy parmesan cheese shell. Linger late over a bottle of wine, inside or out.
☎ 041 275 06 22 ✉ Campiello dell'Anconeta 1828 ❧ 7.30pm–2am 🚢 San Marcuola ⓥ

Gam Gam (4, B2)
Kosher/Mediterranean €€
Gam Gam is great for your taste buds if you like Israeli-style felafels and other Middle Eastern delicacies. This place is fully kosher

and presents a diverse menu, ranging from Red Sea spaghetti to couscous. It also has a set salad buffet (€9.50) and set dish of Israeli appetisers, including falafel (€9).
☎ 041 71 52 84 ✉ Calle del Ghetto Vecchio 1123 ❧ Sun–Thu, lunch Fri 🚢 Guglie 🚹 ⓥ

Mirai (4, B3)
Japanese €€€
The only Japanese restaurant in town, this attractive designer diner with garden is a pleasant setting for a little sushi, sashimi or *uramaki*

(inside-out sushi). Everyone at the Oriental studies faculty must be pleased!
☎ 041 220 65 17 ✉ Lista di Spagna 227 ❧ dinner Tue–Sun 🚢 Ferrovia 🚹

Osteria al Ponte (3, J2)
Osteria €€
This aptly named and highly recommended snack place is on the 'frontier' with Sestiere di Castello. Almost claustrophobically small, it is a well-regarded stop where you can nibble on *cicheti* and indulge in good wines.
☎ 041 528 61 57 ✉ Calle Larga G Gallina 6378 ❧ 8am–8.30pm Mon–Sat 🚢 Fondamente Nuove

Osteria da Alberto (3, H2)
Osteria €€
Another hidden Venetian jewel, this place is run by Alberto, a well-known figure in the business of serving up traditional food in Venice. Be aware that they close the kitchen at about 9pm. The *baccalà* (cod) is good.
☎ 041 523 81 53 ✉ Calle Larga G Gallina 5401 ❧ Mon–Sat 🚢 Ospedale Civile

Osteria dalla Vedova (3, F1)
Osteria €€
The 'Widow's Inn', off Strada Nova, is also called Trattoria Ca' d'Or and is one of the oldest *osterie* in Venice. The food, whether you nibble on the *cicheti* or settle in for a full (mostly seafood) meal, is good and modestly priced.
☎ 041 528 53 24 ✉ Calle del Pistor 3912 ❧ Mon–Wed & Fri–Sat, dinner Sun 🚢 Ca' d'Oro

Osteria da Alberto: the locals know it as Alberto's place

Try the *bigoli* (thick, rough Venetian pasta) at Al Portego

Tre Spiedi da Bes (3, H2)
Venetian €€
Choose from several broths and pasta for the first course and then dig into, say, a slab of sole (fish lords it over the menu) for the main in this congenial Venetian *osteria*, crammed with all sorts of odds and ends hanging on the walls.
☎ 041 520 80 35 ✉ Salizada San Canciano 5906/d 🕑 Tue-Sat & Sun dinner 🚇 Rialto

Vini da Gigio (4, E3)
Restaurant €€€
Gigio stocks a fine selection of reds and whites from the Veneto and beyond, and a trip here means good wine in the company of some excellent cooking. It's a romantically crammed little place. The pasta seafood combinations are among the scrummier options.
☎ 041 528 51 40 ✉ Fondamenta della Chiesa 3628/a 🕑 Wed-Sun 🚇 Ca' d'Oro

CASTELLO

Al Portego (3, H3)
Osteria €€
Situated beneath the portico that gives this *osteria* its name, Al Portego is an inviting stop for *cicheti* and wine, along with some robust meals. Try the *bigoli* (thick, rough Venetian pasta) and whatever sauce they come with.
☎ 041 522 90 38 ✉ Calle Malvasia 6015 🕑 Mon-Sat 🚇 Rialto

Alle Testiere (3, H3)
Trattoria €€€€
The chef may well come for a chat as you sample the tasty offerings in the cosy dining area. Fish is the leitmotif. A handful of starters and pasta courses (all around €16) are followed by a couple of set mains or fresh fish. Round off with quality wines.
☎ 041 522 72 20 ✉ Calle del Mondo Nuovo 5801 🕑 Tue-Sat 🚇 Rialto

Trattoria Corte Sconta

Osteria Santa Marina (3, H3)
Venetian €€€
This *osteria* offers a pleasant dining area and tables on the square. The cuisine is largely a refined take on Venetian seafood dishes and attracts locals and visitors in droves (booking advisable). But the best comes last with exquisite desserts.
☎ 041 528 52 39 🖳 www.osteriadisantamarina.it ✉ Campo Santa Marina 5911 🕑 Tue-Sat, dinner Mon 🚇 Rialto

Trattoria Corte Sconta (2, F4)
Trattoria €€€
A cosy eatery with the option of dining in the rear courtyard, Corte Sconta is well off even the unbeaten track. The chefs prepare almost exclusively seafood classics, such as their delicious *risotto ai scampi*. The owners claim to use only the catch of the day. Who can carp at such a policy? Try the home-made desserts.
☎ 041 522 70 24 ✉ Calle Pestrin 3886 🕑 Tue-Sat Feb–mid-Jul & mid-Aug–Dec 🚇 Arsenale

Trattoria da Remigio (2, F4)
Italian €€
Here is a *trattoria* of the old school. Efficient waiters in jacket and tie glide about the tastefully sober dining rooms serving modestly priced dishes. A broad range of *antipasti* and pasta (€8) first courses are followed by reliable fish and meat mains, such as the *bistecca ai ferri* (grilled steak; €11). Book ahead as it is often full.

☎ 041 523 00 89 ✉ Salizada dei Greci 3416 ☷ Wed-Sun, lunch Mon ⛴ San Zaccaria

GIUDECCA

Ai Tre Scaini (2, E6)
Trattoria €€

In this rambunctious and chaotic *trattoria* you can settle down with ebullient local families for no-nonsense pasta and seafood dishes. Throaty wine comes from a couple of small barrels set up inside. You can eat in the garden, too.

☎ 041 522 47 90 ✉ Calle Michelangelo 53/c ☷ Tue-Wed & Fri-Sun, lunch Mon ⛴ Zitelle ♿

Harry's Dolci (2, C6)
Restaurant/Snack Bar €€€€

Run by Harry's Bar, this place, with tables by the canal looking across to Dorsoduro, has fantastic desserts (which is the main reason for stopping by). It also does full meals and snacks. Dress smartly and expect to part company with at least €100 for a full meal.

☎ 041 522 48 44 ✉ Fondamenta San Biagio 773 ☷ Wed-Mon Apr-Oct ⛴ Palanca ♿

Mistrà (2, D6)
Ligurian & Venetian €€€

Head up the stairs amid the boatyards to this perfect viewpoint across the southern half of the lagoon. Cuisine is an original mix of local and Ligurian dishes, such as the Genovese classic, *trofie al pesto* (slim pasta chunkettes drenched in pesto sauce). Seafood dominates the menu representing two one-time maritime powers.

☎ 041 522 07 43 ✉ Giudecca 212/a ☷ Wed-Sun & lunch Mon ⛴ Redentore

---

CAFÉ CULTURE

- *Espresso* – a small cup of strong black coffee
- *Doppio espresso* – a double espresso
- *Caffè lungo* – watery espresso (long black)
- *Caffè americano* – approximation of filter coffee
- *Caffellatte* – with milk, a breakfast coffee
- *Cappuccino* – frothy version of a *caffellatte*, also a breakfast coffee
- *Caffè macchiato* – espresso with a dash of frothy milk
- *Caffè freddo* – a long glass with cold coffee and ice cubes
- *Corretto* – espresso 'corrected' with grappa or other liquor

---

Get to know the locals at Ai Tre Scaini

Entertainment

Venice, its inhabitants and its visitors constitute a theatrical spectacle in themselves. Good thing, really, because the lagoon city has long shed its 18th-century reputation as Europe's premier pleasure dome.

The student population and steady stream of visitors keep a broad selection of enticing bars active, and there is an extraordinarily broad offering of theatre, opera and dance for such a small town. Do not, however, come to Venice for the clubbing! Things are busy until about 2am, beyond which it's slim pickings.

The reborn Teatro La Fenice (p70) leads the way in the city's busy opera and performing-arts calendar, ably assisted by a handful of other theatres. Most drama is in Italian only. Other music options range from concerts of classical and baroque music to a little jazz or blues in a handful of venues.

There is only one decent cinema in Venice itself and movies tend to be dubbed into Italian. Most locals gorge themselves on a year's worth of films at the annual September film festival.

Indeed, a string of festivals, traditional and arts-oriented – not to mention the glorious Carnevale in February – fill the Venetian calendar. The tourist offices (p88) can provide an updated list of events.

One of the single best sources of bars, cafés, theatre and cinema listings is the monthly bilingual *VeNews* magazine, available at newsstands. Another good source is a freebie distributed in many bars and restaurants, *VDV (Venezia da Vivere)*. Check out www.ombra.net too.

SPECIAL EVENTS

January *Regatta delle Befane* – 6 January; the first of the year's more than 100 regattas, this features rowing Venetian-style *(voga veneta),* which involves various kinds of lagoon boats loosely resembling gondolas, whose crews row standing up.

February *Carnevale* – Venetians don spectacular masks and costumes for this week-long party in the run-up to Ash Wednesday; starting dates for Carnevale in the next few years are 9 February 2007, 25 January 2008 and 13 February 2009 (see also Rites of Spring, p70).

April *Festa di San Marco* – 25 April; on the feast day of the city's patron saint, menfolk give their beloved a bunch of roses.

May *Vogalonga* – some 3000 people and boats of all descriptions (powered by human muscle) participate in the 32km 'long row' from San Marco to Burano and back to the Grand Canal.
Festa della Sensa – second Sunday in May; since AD 998 Venice has marked Ascension Day with the Sposalizio del Mar (Marriage to the Sea), marking the city's relationship with the sea (the mayor takes on the ducal role now); regattas off the Lido.
Palio delle Quattro Antiche Repubbliche Marinare – late May to early June; Amalfi, Genoa, Pisa and Venice take turns to host the Historical Regatta of the Four Ancient Maritime Republics, in which four galleons compete; next in Venice in 2007.

June *Marciliana* – medieval pageant in Chioggia to commemorate the siege of the city by Genoa in 1380; parades and competition, including rowing and archery, between five *contrade* (town quarters).
Sagra di San Pietro in Castello – last weekend in June; busy festival with music, drinking and eating at the steps of the church.
Venezia Biennale Internazionale d'Arte – June to October/November; biennial international exhibition of visual arts held in permanent pavilions near the Giardini Pubblici (2, G5) and other locations throughout the city. An architecture version is held in alternate years.

July *Festa del Redentore* – third weekend in July; pontoon between Dorsoduro and the church of SS Redentore on Giudecca is set up for thanksgiving celebrations for the end of the plague in 1577; regattas, partying on boats and highlight of midnight fireworks extravaganza.

September *Regatta Storica* – first Sunday in September; historic gondola race along the Grand Canal and parade of 15th-century–style boats.
Mostra del Cinema di Venezia – annual Venice International Film Festival, Italy's version of Cannes, held at the Palazzo del Cinema on the Lido.

November *Festa della Madonna della Salute* – 21 November; procession on pontoon across the Grand Canal to the church of Santa Maria della Salute to give thanks for the city's deliverance from plague in 1630.

BARS

The liveliest areas for bars are in and around the young and bustling Campo Santa Margherita in Dorsoduro (3, B4), around the Rialto markets (3, G2) and along Fondamenta degli Ormesini (4, C1) and Fondamenta della Misericordia (4, D2) in Cannaregio. More traditional wine bars *(bacari)* generally close fairly early.

Ai Do Draghi (3, B4)
You can't get much smaller than this colourful, old-time *bacaro,* perfect for a red wine or *spritz: prosecco* (light sparkling white wine), soda water and bitter. Beyond the cube of a timber-lined bar is a rear sitting area, but most of the time punters mill around outside or grab a table in the *campo.*
☎ 041 528 97 31 ✉ Calle della Chiesa, Dorsoduro 3665 ⏰ 7.30am-2am Fri-Wed 🚤 Ca' Rezzonico

Al Bottegon (Cantina di Vini già Schiavi; 2, D5)
Wander into this fusty old wine bar for a glass of *prosecco* beneath the bar's low-slung rafters and in the wavering light provided by dodgy bulbs. Locals have been doing just that for countless decades.
☎ 041 523 00 34 ✉ Fondamenta Maravegie, Dorsoduro 992 ⏰ 8.30am-8.30pm Mon-Sat 🚤 Zattere

Aurora (3, H5)
Venice's funkiest new bar is a slice of a bigger town right at the heartbeat of conventional Venice. A chilled lounge has taken up residence in what by day is a historic café. Local DJs and performers inject sparkle into the evening, nicely oiled with colourful, if rather pricey (as much as €10 to €12), cocktails.
☎ 041 528 64 05 ✉ Piazza San Marco 48-50 ⏰ 8pm-2am Wed-Sun 🚤 Vallaresso & San Marco

B Bar (3, G5)
You may not be able to afford a night in the Bauer, one of the city's top hotels, but a little splurge in its B Bar is worth considering. This elegant, ground-floor cocktail bar is ideal for a stylish tipple, and with luck you'll find a spot overlooking the Grand Canal.
☎ 041 520 70 22 ✉ Campo San Moisè, San Marco 1455 ⏰ 6.30pm-3am Wed-Sun 🚤 Vallaresso & San Marco

Bacaro Lounge (3, G5)
This vibrant oval bar next to the Mondadori bookstore vibrates with an early evening dynamism. Locals engage in busy banter over a cocktail before heading for a meal in the restaurant up the glass stairway, or perhaps a reading in the bookshop.
☎ 041 296 06 87 ✉ Salizada San Moisè, San Marco 1348 ⏰ 9am-2am 🚤 Vallaresso & San Marco

Bagolo (3, D2)
With its timber floors and low lighting inside, and candlelit tables outside, this laid-back drinkery lends a muted nocturnal buzz to this pretty square.
☎ 041 71 75 84 ✉ Campo San Giacomo dell'Orio, Santa Croce 1584 ⏰ 7am-midnight Sep-Apr, 7am-2am May-Aug 🚤 Riva de Biasio

Café Noir (3, C4)
You can start the day with breakfast in here or hang out into the night with a mixed crowd of Italian students and foreigners. As the name suggests, with the exception of red lampshades, the place is largely black.
☎ 041 71 09 25 ✉ Calle San Pantalon, Dorsoduro 3805 ⏰ 7am-2am Mon-Sat 🚤 San Tomà

Caffè (3, B4)
At the heart of the scene on Campo Santa Margherita

If the walls of Al Bottegon could talk...

If you see a lost Caffè waitress, please send her home

is this perennially overcrowded student haunt. Known affectionately to locals as the *caffè rosso* (the 'red café') because of the colour of its sign, it draws a happily hip crowd for snacks and drinks.

☎ 041 528 79 98 ✉ Campo Santa Margherita, Dorsoduro 2693 ⏰ 7am-1am Mon-Sat 🚤 Ca' Rezzonico

Caffè Blue (3, C3)
Although quiet on weekday evenings, this coolish and cramped student bar gets busy at weekends, especially

when it puts on a little live music. As the night wears on, drinkers pour out onto the streets outside (despite this not being permitted).

☎ 041 71 02 27 ✉ Calle dei Preti, Dorsoduro 3778 ⏰ 8am-2pm & 5pm-2am Mon-Sat 🚤 San Tomà

Centrale (3, G5)
The international, switched-on ambience in this bar (and restaurant), which would be equally at home in London's Shoreditch, throbs softly to chill-out and lounge sounds in a 21st-century establishment.

☎ 041 296 06 64 💻 www .centrale-lounge.com ✉ Piscina di Frezzaria, San Marco 1659/b ⏰ 6.30pm-2am Mon-Sat 🚤 Vallaresso & San Marco

Dogado (4, E3)
The best part of this elegant bar-restaurant is swinging in the garden chairs on the summer roof terrace with a cocktail (€9) or one of an unending variety of imported beers in hand. The dark, modern timber furnishings and candlelight inside are

just as tempting in the colder months.

☎ 041 520 85 44 ✉ Strada Nova, Cannaregio 3660/a ⏰ 11am-1.30am 🚤 Ca d'Oro

Harry's Bar (3, G5)
As well as being a noted restaurant (p53), Harry's is, of course, first and foremost a bar. Everyone who is anyone and passing through Venice usually ends up here. Characters as diverse as Orson Welles and Truman Capote have sipped on a cocktail or two at Harry's.

☎ 041 528 57 77 ✉ Calle Vallaresso, San Marco 1323 ⏰ noon-11pm 🚤 Vallaresso & San Marco

Improntacafé (3, C4)
A snazzy snack bar and restaurant by day, this place comes into its own as a be-seen-in wine bar with food in the evening. Sidle up to the bar for a goblet of fine Italian wine by the glass (€2.50 to €4) or opt for a light sit-down meal and order a bottle!

☎ 041 275 03 86 ✉ Calle Crosera, Dorsoduro 3815 ⏰ 7am-2am Mon-Sat 🚤 San Tomà

Margaret Duchamp (3, B4)
Margaret Duchamp is set at a strategic angle and is perennially popular with a mixed crowd of locals, students and blow-ins. Perfect for seeing and being seen, and equally popular for the *aperitivo* and late-night drinking and music.

☎ 041 528 62 55 ✉ Campo Santa Margherita, Dorsoduro 3019

MAKE MINE CAMPARI
In a country not noted for heavy drinkers, Venetians form a category all their own. Locals can often be seen indulging in alcoholic cardiac stimulation at breakfast time and few skip the chance for a *prosecco* (light sparkling white wine) or two at some point in the day. Early evening is *aperitivo* time, and the favoured beverage is the *spritz* (*prosecco*, soda water and bitter – Campari, Amaro, Aperol or Select), one of the few things introduced by the Austrians in the 19th century that the Venetians appreciated. Later on, locals do not disdain a couple of classic Venetian cocktails, such as the Bellini (champagne or *prosecco* and peach nectar).

Margaret Duchamp: perfect for seeing and being seen

🕒 10am-2am Wed-Mon
🚢 Ca' Rezzonico

Muro Vino e Cucina (3, G2)
Along with the snazzy, avant-garde restaurant upstairs, this unusually hip, urban ground-floor bar attracts a small, select crowd in search of a modern ambience.
☎ 041 523 74 95
✉ Campo Cesare Battisti, San Polo 222 🕒 4pm-1am Mon-Sat 🚢 Rialto

Orange (3, B5)
The colour of an Aperol *spritz*, Orange appeals to a beautiful crowd that identifies with the fashion videos playing constantly. Skip the lurid bar and head out the back to the pleasant garden.
☎ 041 523 47 40
✉ Campo Santa Margherita, Dorsoduro 3054/a
🕒 8am-2am 🚢 Ca' Rezzonico

Osteria agli Ormesini (4, C1)
Oodles of wine and 120 types of bottled beer in one knockabout place? Perhaps you should get along to this *osteria*. It's something of a student haunt for those who like gruff service, a no-nonsense ambience and an amazing choice of ambers.
☎ 041 71 58 34
✉ Fondamenta degli Ormesini, Cannaregio 2710
🕒 7.30pm-2am Mon-Sat
🚢 Madonna dell'Orto

Paradiso Perduto (4, D2)
Venice's young and restless are still drawn to this barn of a place although the great food for which it was known is a thing of the past. Tables outside are appealing in summer, while the cavernous interior is perfect for rowdy tippling and the occasional live act.
☎ 041 72 05 81 ✉ Fondamenta della Misericordia 2540 🕒 7pm-2am Thu-Mon
🚢 Madonna dell'Orto

Taverna da Baffo (3, D2)
Named after Casanova's licentious poet pal Giorgio Baffo and lined with his rhymes in praise of 'the round arse' and other female anatomical attributes, this bar has a chirpy feel. In summer the tables outside are especially pleasant for *spritz* sipping.
☎ 041 520 88 62
✉ Campiello Sant'Agostin, Dorsoduro 2346
🕒 7.30am-2am Mon-Fri, 5pm-2am Sat-Sun 🚢 San Tomà

Torino@Notte (3, G4)
Cunningly disguised as a busy but standard Venetian café by day, this place is transfigured at night by a lively student crowd and foreign interlopers. They herd in for mixed tipples and loudish music, and on the odd occasion even a live gig.
☎ 041 522 39 14
✉ Campo San Luca, San Marco 4592 🕒 8pm-1am Tue-Sat 🚢 Rialto

Vitae (Il Muro; 3, F4)
Il Muro (the wall) is busy by day with a lunchtime tippling crowd and again late on a Friday or Saturday night, when little else is happening in this part of town – it's a lively beacon of hedonism. The best time to pop by is for after-work drinks around 7pm to 10pm.
☎ 041 520 52 05 ✉ Calle San Antonio, San Marco 4118 🕒 9am-1am Mon-Fri, 9am-2am Sat 🚢 Vallaresso & San Marco

Zanzibar (3, J3)
This crooked kiosk looks set to crumble into the canal and provides great life-theatre entertainment. Pull up a seat on the square and settle in for a few people-watching drinks to the thumping music emanating from the bar.
☎ 339 200 68 31 ✉ Fondamenta Santa Maria Formosa, Castello 5840
🕒 9am-1am 🚢 Rialto

CLUBS & CASINOS

Clubbing in Venice itself is virtually nonexistent. A handful of places have late licences and small dance spaces. Mestre (5, B1) offers a few clubs and in summer the action takes place at the Lido di Jesolo (1, E2) – keep an eye on *VeNews* for details.

You bet your *palazzo* it's a casino!

Casinò Municipale di Venezia (4, D3)

Housed in the Renaissance Palazzo Vendramin-Calergi, where the composer Richard Wagner passed on in 1883, here the gambler will find all his or her old favourites, from slot machines to roulette. Jackets obligatory (and available on loan).

☎ 041 529 71 11 🖳 www .casinovenezia.it ✉ Palazzo Vendramin-Calergi, Cannaregio 2040 € €10

🕙 3.30pm-2.30am 🚊 San Marcuola

Cielo

In four dance spaces in this club near Marco Polo airport, locals indulge in anything from house to Latin rhythms or mainstream pop. The place seems to be in a constant state of name and theme change.

☎ 041 541 51 00 ✉ Via Ca' Zorzi 2, Tessera 🕙 9pm-4am Thu & Sat 🚌 Nos 5 & 55 or taxi

Club Malvasia Vecchia (3, E5)

This social club functions as a late-night bar and dance den beloved of students and a hip, artsy crowd; about the best option after 2am in all Venice.

☎ 041 522 58 83 ✉ Corte Malatina, San Marco 2586 € one-off membership fee €15 🕙 11pm-4am Fri & Sat 🚊 Santa Maria del Giglio

Magic Bus

Big and popular, Magic Bus administers a diet of anything from '90s rock to electronic sounds and occasionally stages live concerts.

☎ 041 595 21 51 🖳 www .magicbus.it ✉ Via delle Industrie 118, Marcon, Mestre € €8-10 🕙 11pm-5am Fri & Sat 🚊 Mestre, then taxi

QuotAmare (5, E3)

The hot summer spot on the Lido beach, QuotAmare brings some of the sunny club scene of Ibiza to the Old Lady of the Lagoon. Stylish, perma-tanned folks sip cocktails and let rip to club sounds on the beach until late into the night (especially Friday and Saturday).

☎ 393 801 29 10 🖳 www .quotAmare.com ✉ Lido

GAY & LESBIAN VENICE

Virtually nothing is done to cater specifically for gays and lesbians in Venice, though you could head for the handful of places in Mestre and Padua. In Mestre, try **Metrò Venezia** (5, B1; ☎ 041 538 42 99; www.metroclub.it; Via Cappuccina 82/b; admission €15; 🕙 2pm-2am), with several sauna and massage rooms, bar and dark room. In Padua, half a dozen bars cater to the gay scene, including **Flexo Video Bar** (☎ 049 807 47 07; www.flexoclub.it; Via Tommaseo 96a). The city's one gay club, **Black & White** (☎ 049 738 97 91; www.black-disco.com; Viale della Navigazione Interna 49b), is in the industrial outskirts of town.

di Venezia ⏲ 7am–2am
Jun–mid-Sep 🚊 Lido

Round Midnight (3, B5)

Not quite a club but more than a bar, this back-canal drink and dance den keeps punters from Campo Santa Margherita happy in the wee small hours when all else closes. A mix of acid jazz, Latin and sometimes rockier sounds predominates. Opening times can be erratic – we have seen it in full swing in mid-July.

☎ 041 523 20 56 ✉ Fondamenta dello Squero, Dorsoduro 3102 € €5 ⏲ midnight–4am Mon-Sat Sep–May 🚊 Ca' Rezzonico

The Blu Rooms

A one-time factory now maintains an industrial feel with its great sheet windows and exposed tubes, combined with a baroque decadence in its chandeliers and red curtains. Rock up for house sessions on Friday and classic mainstream pop, home-grown and international, on Saturday.

☎ 041 538 49 83 🖳 www .blunotte.it ✉ Via delle Industrie 29, Marghera ⏲ Fri-Sat 🚉 Mestre, then taxi 🅿

LIVE MUSIC, PERFORMING ARTS & CINEMA

Apart from those listed below, several smaller theatres are scattered about Venice, Mestre and the hinterland. Just as the grand opera theatre Teatro La Fenice has emerged from its scaffolding, the city's main drama stage, the Teatro Goldoni (3, G3), has been covered up for a makeover. If you're interested in baroque theatre, musical ensembles dressed in billowing 18th-century costume regularly perform concerts of baroque and light classical music from about Easter to the end of September. Clearly these shows are aimed at tourists and can be cheesy but the musical quality is not necessarily bad.

A handful of places – eateries and bars like Paradiso Perduto (p66) and Caffè Blue (p65) – intermittently put on live music, usually jazz, blues and mild pop. Watch the local press for annual events in Jesolo (1, E2) and Marghera (5, B1).

The cinema scene is limited in Venice and you will be unlikely to see anything in English. In July and August a big screen is erected in Campo San Polo, which makes for one of the more magical settings for outdoor cinema.

Al Vapore (5, B1)

About the best place for a consistent programme of jazz, blues and other music, Al

The restored Teatro La Fenice (p70): a new lease of life for Venice's *grande dame* of opera

Catch an opera at the 17th-century Teatro Malibran (p70)

Vapore is in Marghera, on the mainland. The club occasionally attracts good foreign acts as well as local talent.
☎ 041 93 07 96 🖳 www .alvapore.it ✉ Via Fratelli Bandiera 8, Marghera € varies 🕙 7pm-2am Tue-Sun 🚊 Mestre or bus 6, 6B, 66 & N2

Arsenale (2, G4)
Since the early 2000s La Biennale organisers have run several small theatre spaces in disused parts of the once mighty Venetian shipyards (p26). They include the Teatro alle Tese, Tese delle Vergini, Corderie dell'Arsenale, Spazio Fonderie and Teatro Piccolo Arsenale.
☎ 041 521 87 75 🖳 www .labiennale.org ✉ Arsenale, Castello 🚊 Arsenale

Cinema Giorgione Movie d'Essai (3, G1)
The Giorgione is a comparatively modern cinema complex which presents a reasonable range of decent movies.
☎ 041 522 62 98 ✉ Rio Terà Franceschi, Cannaregio

4612 🕙 2 or 3 sessions (around 4pm, 6pm & 9.15pm) 🚊 Fondamente Nuove 🚹

Interpreti Veneziani
Since the mid-1980s this group has been presenting concerts of, above all, Venetian music in the church of San Vidal (3, E5). Vivaldi, of course, heads the list but the musicians handle other Italian masters and the occasional interloper like Bach. They have performed as far afield as the Bayreuth festival and Melbourne, Australia. They are one of several more or less cheesy baroque music ensembles that perform mostly for tourists.
☎ 041 277 05 61 🖳 www.interpretiven eziani.com ✉ Chiesa San Vidal, Campo San Vidal, San Marco 2862/b € €22/17 🚊 Accademia

Musica a Palazzo
Welcome to the 19th century. Climb the stairs to this noble mansion (Palazzo Barbarigo-Minotto; 3, E6) on the Grand Canal for an

enchanting and unique evening. Take up a seat in the salon and later the master bedroom for operatic duos and delicious excerpts of light classical music. On some evenings they present *La Traviata*, moving from one room to another. Rarely can one experience opera in so intimate a fashion and in such a setting, in a grand Venetian mansion laden with stucco and original Tiepolos.
☎ 340 971 7272 🖳 www .musicapalazzo.com ✉ Fondamenta Barbarigo o Duodo, San Marco 2504 € €40 🕙 8.30pm 🚊 Santa Maria del Giglio

Teatro Goldoni (3, G3)
Named after Venice's version of Shakespeare, Carlo Goldoni, this is the city's main drama theatre, although it often stages concerts and other entertainment.
☎ 041 240 20 11 🖳 www .teatrostabileveneto.it ✉ Calle Teatro Goldoni, San Marco 4650/b € €7-30 🚊 Rialto

RITES OF SPRING

Venetians have been celebrating the approach of spring with Carnevale (Carnival) since the 15th century. In those days private clubs organised masked balls, and popular entertainment included bull-baiting and firing live dogs from cannons! By the 18th century, Venice was home to hedonism and the licentious goings-on of Carnevale lasted for two months.

Things quietened down after the city's fall to Napoleon in 1797. Revived in 1979, Carnevale has since become the world's best-known baroque fancy-dress party, as extravagant as Rio's Carnival is riotous.

The festivities begin on a Friday afternoon (dates move around – see Special Events, p63) with a procession, followed by the official start with a traditional masked procession from Piazza San Marco around 4pm.

The following Thursday is Giovedì Grasso (Fat Thursday) and Friday afternoon's highlight is the Gran Ballo delle Maschere (Grand Masked Ball) in Piazza San Marco.

Saturday and Sunday are given over to musical and theatrical performances in Piazza San Marco. Also, on the Sunday, a slew of decorated boats and gondolas bearing masked passengers wends its way serenely down the Grand Canal.

The event winds up with a parade of the Re del Carnevale (Carnival King) and the one-time guilds of the city.

Teatro La Fenice (3, F5)
Venice's grand opera theatre is an experience music lovers will not want to miss. The theatre has been restored to its former glory and equipped with the latest technology. First-night spots can cost several thousand euros. Some operas are staged at the 17th-century **Teatro Malibran** (3, H2; Calle del Teatro, San Marco 5870; €10 to €95) instead.
☎ 041 78 65 11 🖳 www
.teatrolafenice.it ✉ Campo San Fantin, San Marco 1977 € €20-1000 🚤 Santa Maria del Giglio

SPORT

Football

Tickets to see the local football side, **SSC Venezia** (☎ 041 238 07 11; www .veneziacalcio.it), play are available at the Stadio Penzo (2, H6) at the eastern tip of the city and from Vela outlets such as those in front of the train station (3, A1 and 3, B1). They can cost around €15 to €20. Getting a ticket on the day is rarely a problem as this side generally muddles along in Serie B (second division) or even Serie C (third division), which it led in 2006.

Rowing & Sailing

Venetians love to get out onto the lagoon in one form of vessel or other. Rowing and sailing regattas dot the city calendar and the keen can even have a go themselves (see Row Your Boat, p34).

Carnevale: the world's best-known baroque fancy-dress party

Sleeping

The lagoon mini-metropolis is jam-packed with hundreds of digs of all possible descriptions. They range from simple, family-run establishments to the luxurious honey pots that draw celebs. Quality varies enormously and price does not always guarantee it. It is possible to find romantic rooms with ceiling frescoes in centuries-old *palazzi* (mansions) for much less than 'clinical' rooms in some of the grander-sounding places.

ROOM RATES

The categories indicate the cost per night of a standard double room in high season.

Deluxe	from €400
Top End	€251-399
Midrange	€121-250
Budget	up to €120

San Clemente Palace (p72)

The hotels around Piazza San Marco generally charge extraordinary sums, especially when they look out over the Grand Canal or Bacino di San Marco. A bevy of budget hotels, convenient but frequently uninspiring, is cluttered around Rio Terà Lista di Spagna (4, A3), which leads from the train station towards the centre.

Increasingly, quality budget options, along with an array of midrange and some grander places (among them a veritable explosion of tempting B&Bs since the late 1990s), are spread further away from these standard poles of attention, in quieter corners of districts such as Dorsoduro, Santa Croce and Cannaregio.

Hotels go by other names too. The Italian *albergo* means hotel, while a *locanda* or *pensione* usually indicates a more modest, family-run establishment.

Space is at a premium. Rooms are often small, even at pricey spots. In most upper-level hotels you can expect a standard array of amenities: phone, TV (often satellite), minibar, safe, air-con, en suite bathroom with hairdryer, internet connection and 24-hour service. Only a few can offer extras such as pools. Midrange places tend to offer only the phone, TV and air-con. Rooms in cheaper locales often have only a washbasin, with a shared bathroom along the corridor.

Single travellers frequently get stung, as many hotels offer double rooms at only slightly reduced rates to loners.

Some hotels close in winter, especially those on the Lido, often shut from November to April. Finding a room on the Lido during the September film festival requires advance booking.

DELUXE

Ca' Maria Adele (2, E5)
You'd never guess at the discreet luxury inside this 16th-century pleasure dome of 14 rooms. Five are themed – eg the Doge's (Duke's) Room – while others display rich tapestries and dark timber ceilings.
☎ 041 520 30 78 💻 www.camariaadele.it ✉ Rio Terà Catecumeni, Dorsoduro 111 🚤 Salute 🍴 Linea d'Ombra (p54)

Cipriani (2, E6)
Set in the one-time villa of the noble Mocenigo family and surrounded by lavish grounds, the Cipriani has unbeatable views across to San Marco and an elite feel. You can dine excellently in the hotel restaurant and a private launch runs between the hotel and San Marco.
☎ 041 520 77 44 💻 www.hotelcipriani.it ✉ Giudecca 10 🚤 Zitelle 🍴 Fortuny Restaurant, Cip's Club, Fortuny Terrace & Gabbiano Poolside Restaurants 🚼

San Clemente Palace (5, D3)
The rose-coloured buildings of the one-time monastery

BOOK ACCOMMODATION ONLINE
For more recommendations by Lonely Planet authors, check out the online booking service at www.lonelyplanet.com.

and madhouse of San Clemente make a unique setting. The hotel has 205 rooms and suites, two swimming pools, tennis courts, a golf course and wonderful gardens. Oh, and central Venice is just a private launch ride away.
☎ 041 244 50 01 💻 www.thi.it ✉ Isola San Clemente 🚤 private shuttle from San Zaccaria 🍴 Ca' dei Frati, Le Maschere & La Laguna 🚼

TOP END

Ca' Pisani Hotel (3, D6)
Named after a 14th-century Venetian hero, this centuries-old building houses a self-conscious Design Hotel filled with 1930s and '40s furnishings and plenty of specially made items. The rooms, some with exposed-beam ceilings, are full of pleasing decorative touches.
☎ 041 240 14 11 💻 www.capisanihotel.it ✉ Rio Terà Antonio Foscarini, Dorsoduro 979a 🚤 Accademia 🍴 La Rivista

DD.724 (3, E6)
A wealth of modern design and contemporary art touches lies behind the surly walls of these acutely modern designer digs. The seven rooms and suites are individually tailored, with features like LCD TV and home cinema. It looks onto the gardens of the Peggy Guggenheim Collection.
☎ 041 277 02 62 💻 www.dd724.it ✉ Dorsoduro 724 🚤 Accademia 🍴 Ai Gondolieri (p54)

Hotel Monaco & Grand Canal (3, G5)
This elegant 17th-century *palazzo* on the Grand Canal is a brisk stroll from Piazza San Marco. Owned by the Benetton family, it oozes an easy elegance. The rooms overlooking the canal are the most sought after and the canalside terrace is magnificent.
☎ 041 520 02 11 💻 www.summithotels.com ✉ San Marco 1325 🚤 San Marco & Vallaresso 🍴 Terrace & Grand Canal Restaurant

Hotel San Cassiano (3, F1)
The 14th-century Ca' Favretto houses a selection of rooms; the best are high-ceilinged doubles overlooking the Grand Canal. The building is a wonderful old pile, with stone doorways along the staircases.
☎ 041 524 17 68 💻 www.sancassiano.it ✉ Calle della Rosa, Santa Croce

Cipriani: one-time villa of the noble Mocenigo family

2232 🚉 San Stae 🍴 Vecio Fritolin (p58)

Palazzo Priuli (2, F4)
The 14th-century Palazzo Priuli (home to several *doges*) occupies a privileged position by the Ponte del Diavolo (Devil's Bridge) and oozes much of its past glory. Smallish standard rooms are elegantly decorated, with high ceilings, exposed timber and brickwork.
☎ 041 277 08 34
🖳 www.hotelpriuli .com ✉ Fondamenta dell'Osmarin, Castello 4979 🚉 San Zaccaria 🍴 Trattoria da Remigio (p60)

MIDRANGE

Albergo Accademia Villa Maravege (3, C5)
Set in gorgeous gardens by the Grand Canal and not far from the Gallerie dell'

Accademia, this 17th-century villa has simple, elegant rooms, some with four-poster beds and timber floors. Most look onto the gardens and some have canal glimpses.
☎ 041 521 01 88 🖳 www .pensioneaccademia.it ✉ Fondamenta Bollani, Dorsoduro 1058 🚉 Accademia 🍴 Enoteca Ai Artisti (p54)

Ca' Angeli (3, E3)
A rambling family townhouse, this exquisite spot offers a variety of rooms, the best a generous suite overlooking the Grand Canal. Antique furniture and Murano lamps are scattered throughout. Flop in the canalside reading room. (Note they don't accept credit cards.)
☎ 041 523 24 80 🖳 www .caangeli.it ✉ Calle del Traghetto de la Madonneta, San Polo 1434 🚉 San

Silvestro 🍴 Antiche Carampane (p55)

Ca' La Corte (3, J2)
This 16th-century house gathers around a pleasant inner *corte* (courtyard) with private well. Spacious rooms (some featuring traditional *terrazzo alla veneziana* floors) with exposed ceiling beams are decorated in luxurious Venetian style. One door from the breakfast room leads right onto the Rio di San Marina canal.
☎ 041 241 13 30 🖳 www .locandalacorte.it ✉ Calle Bressana, Castello 6317 🚉 Fondamente Nuove 🍴 Osteria al Ponte (p59)

Ca' Pozzo (4, B2)
Down a narrow alley lurks this little designer spark with contemporary touches (flat-screen TVs, and safes to store a laptop). Clean-lined rooms are individually decorated, each with modern art. Lovers of fusty, old-style Venetian lodgings should not come to this crisp and refreshing hotel.
☎ 041 524 05 04 🖳 www .capozzovenice.com ✉ Sotoportego Ca' Pozzo, Cannaregio 1279 🚉 Guglie 🍴 Gam Gam (p59)

Ca' San Giorgio (4, C3)
Dating at least in part to the 14th century, this family-run spot boasts half a dozen rooms that have been carved out of the Gothic framework. The best is the top floor suite with sloping timber ceiling and *altana* (roof terrace) to enjoy on a sunny morn.
☎ 041 275 91 77 🖳 www .casangiorgio.com ✉ Salizada del Fontego dei Turchi, Santa Croce 1725 🚉 San Stae 🍴 Il Refolo (p57)

TOP DESIGN DIGS
- Ca' Pisani Hotel (opposite)
- DD.724 (opposite)
- Palazzo Soderini (p75)
- Ca' Pozzo (right)

Ca' Pisani Hotel: a showcase of 1930s and '40s design

Hotel Monaco & Grand Canal (p72): 17th-century opulence

Hotel Flora (3, F5)

A quiet three-storey hotel with an Art Nouveau centrepiece staircase, leafy breakfast garden and a mix of 19th-century style and contemporary, creamy-décor rooms, this is a pleasant deal in the core of San Marco.
☎ 041 520 58 44 ⌨ www .hotelflora.it ✉ Calle dei Bergamaschi, San Marco 2283a ⌘ San Marco & Vallaresso

La Calcina (2, D5)

John Ruskin wrote *The Stones of Venice* in this homely hotel, which has a smidgen of garden attached. The immaculate rooms are sober but charming with small terraces or views. Dine on the pontoon set on the canal.
☎ 041 520 64 66 ⌨ www .lacalcina.com ✉ Fondamenta Zattere ai Gesuati, Dorsoduro 780 ⌘ Zattere ✗ La Piscina

Locanda Cipriani (5, E1)

Hemingway loved this out-of-the-way spot, where he would drink and write through the night and then hunt ducks by day. Stay overnight in one of the six spacious, tranquil and tasteful rooms at this country-lagoon getaway.
☎ 041 73 01 50 ⌨ www .locandacipriani.com ✉ Piazza Santa Fosca 29, Torcello ⌘ Torcello ✗ Locanda Cipriani ⌘

Locanda Leon Bianco (3, G2)

Up from an airless courtyard you chance upon this centuries-old jewel. The best three (of eight) rooms look onto the Grand Canal. The undulating floors, heavy timber doors and original locks lend the rooms a timeless charm.
☎ 041 523 35 72 ⌨ www .leonbianco.it ✉ Campiello Leon Bianco, Cannaregio 5629

⌘ Ca' d'Oro ✗ Osteria dalla Vedova (p59)

Locanda Orseolo (3, G4)

Tucked away in a closed courtyard and with views from nine of its 15 rooms (over three floors) over the Bacino Orseolo, a gondola terminal behind Piazza San Marco, this ancient house is run by amiable young staff. Rooms have been painstakingly renovated and decorated and breakfast is made for lingering.
☎ 041 520 48 77 ⌨ www .locandaorseolo.com ✉ Corte Zorzi, San Marco 1083 ⌘ San Marco & Vallaresso ✗ Enoteca Il Volto (p53)

Novecento (3, E5)

East meets West in Venice, and no more so than in this nine-room boutique beauty near the Grand Canal. Its cosy public spaces ooze Oriental opulence. Rooms are a blend of the exotic (beautiful timber beds of a mixed Mediterranean and Far Eastern flavour) and modern comfort.
☎ 041 241 37 65 ⌨ www .novecento.biz ✉ Calle del Dose da Ponte, San

La Calcina charm

APARTMENT LIVING

For many, living locally (if only for a few days or a week) means taking an apartment. Nothing better to feel a trifle more like a local than having your own address. Many agencies offer anything from modest options in remote back lanes to palatial nobles' rooms on the Grand Canal. Among those worth checking out:

- www.venice-rentals.com
- www.visitvenice.co.uk
- www.bellinitravel.com
- www.dimoraveneziana.com
- www.guestinitaly.com
- www.carefree-italy.com

Marco 2683/84 🚤 San Marco & Vallaresso

Oltre il Giardino (3, D3)
This beautifully relaxed home with canalside garden and just six exquisite rooms is a charmer. Timber and parquet floors, elegant furniture and smooth service make it a top choice.
☎ 041 275 00 15 🖳 www .oltreilgiardino-venezia.com ✉ Fondamenta Contarini, San Polo 2542 🚤 San Tomà ✖ Frary's (p56)

Palazzo Soderini (2, F4)
Those detergent ads singing 'whiter than white' spring to mind, for behind the walls of this grand *palazzo* lie modern white (or cream) rooms with minimalist décor. This strict neutrality is offset by a lovely garden and rare splashes of colour in the furniture and bed covers.
☎ 041 296 08 23 🖳 www .palazzosoderini.it ✉ Campo Bandiera e Moro, Castello 3611 🚤 Arsenale ✖ Trattoria Corte Sconta (p60)

BUDGET

Antica Locanda Montin (3, C6)
On a quiet back canal near busy Campo Santa Margherita, this place has been in business since the 1800s and the cosy rooms look either onto the canal or the rear garden. The rear pergola-covered dining area is enticing.
☎ 041 522 71 51 🖳 locandamontin@libero .it ✉ Fondamenta di Borgo, Dorsoduro 1147 🚤 Accademia ✖ Antica Locanda Montin

Hotel Galleria (3, D6)
Hotel Galleria is the only one-star hotel right on the Grand Canal, near the Ponte dell'Accademia. Space is tight, but the homey décor is welcoming. If you snare one of the rooms on the canal, you'll enjoy views others pay a fortune for.
☎ 041 523 24 89 🖳 www .hotelgalleria.it ✉ Rio Terà Antonio Foscarini, Dorsoduro 878/a 🚤 Accademia ✖ Ai Gondolieri (p54)

Locanda Casa Petrarca (3, G4)
A family-run place with simple but sparkling rooms in an ancient apartment building, this is one of the nicest budget places in the San Marco area, tucked away down an alley ending on a canal. Doubles overlooking the canal are more expensive than the standard ones.
☎ 041 520 04 30 ✉ Calle delle Schiavine, San Marco 4386 🚤 San Marco, Vallaresso & Rialto

Pensione Guerrato (3, F2)
Amid the Rialto Markets, this *pensione* is a rare one-star gem, with some rooms enjoying glimpses of the Grand Canal. Housed in a former convent, the rooms display antique furniture, some fragments of centuries-old frescoes and buckets of charm.
☎ 041 528 59 27 🖳 http:// web.tiscalinet.it/pen sioneguerrato ✉ Calle drio la Scimia, San Polo 240/a 🚤 Rialto ✖ Cantina Do Mori (p56)

Pensione Guerrato: a rare one-star gem

About Venice

HISTORY
A Swampy Refuge

Venice, it is claimed, was founded on a string of straggly malarial islets in the Venetian lagoon in AD 421. In 452, Attila the Hun and his marauding armies crashed into northeast Italy (aka the Veneto) and sent its inhabitants fleeing to the lagoon. It was a pattern that would be repeated, and in 726 (some sources say 697) the island communities came together under their first *doge* (duke). By the 9th century the administrative centre had become the islands around Rivo Alto (today's Rialto). Over the succeeding centuries, by reclaiming land and creating artificial islands on beds of timber pylons, the Rivo Alto and its islands took on the present shape of Venice (Venezia), as it became known in the 12th century.

> **MARCO'S MILLIONS**
> When Marco Polo (1254–1324) returned home after more than 20 years in the Far East, he and his travelling father and uncle should have been filthy rich. Their millions were largely stolen in Trabzon, modern Turkey, and instead Marco came to be known for his far-fetched travel tales, which all Venice knew as Il Milione (because there were so many stories). He set them down on paper while in a Genoese prison after being captured in battle; he was released in 1300.

Venice Victorious

By 1095, when the First Crusade was called to liberate the Holy Lands from the Muslims, Venice had consolidated itself as an oligarchic republic under an elected *doge*.

Much of the city's power came from its ownership of territories in Dalmatia, Greece, the mainland and trading bases beyond. Venice ignored the sensibilities of other Christian powers and courted whichever powers it pleased, including Muslim centres from Córdoba to Damascus.

The city's wily ambassadors attempted to keep sweet as many parties as possible, a game that led both Western European powers and

Overlooking Bacino di San Marco, the Lion of St Mark catches angelic utterances on the breeze

Byzantium to be suspicious of the slippery lagoon city. Rival Italian sea powers, especially Genoa, were a constant source of competition, and in 1380 the Genoese attempted a siege of Venice only 30 years after the city had been decimated by the plague of 1348.

Through it all the Venetians continued to extend their power, and by the time Constantinople fell to the Ottoman Turks in 1453, Venice had reached the height of its power. It ruled the Adriatic as a private lake, controlled strategic islands in Greece and held a mainland empire that stretched from Friuli in the east to Bergamo in the west.

Decline, Occupation & Unity

As the 15th century closed, the pressures on Venice grew. Turkey began to nibble away at the city's possessions and Venice could do little while the West remained disunited. Indeed, la Serenissima (Venice) found itself on occasion fighting the Turks *and* Western powers.

The rounding of the Cape of Good Hope by the Portuguese at the end of the 15th century boded ill for Venetian trade, as did the rise of vigorous nation states like England and France. The fall of Crete to the Turks in the late 17th century was a further hammer blow.

Venice clung to its mainland possessions but by the 18th century had lost its appetite for struggle. Venice came to be known throughout Europe as a party town, although its own noble class was becoming increasingly destitute. Carnevale (see Rites of Spring, p70, for the modern version) lasted as long as two months, casinos did a roaring trade and Venetian prostitutes of every class were rarely short of clients.

The end of the Republic could not have been more ignominious. Napoleon marched into northern Italy in the late 1790s in pursuit of Austrian forces and swaggered into Piazza San Marco without firing a shot. The city subsequently ended up in Austrian hands until 1866, the year Venice joined the newly formed Kingdom of Italy.

The late 19th century saw a resurgence in trade and industrial activity on Giudecca (the biggest remnant is the Mulino Stucky, which is being turned into a hotel and congress complex) and the mainland. The beginning of tourism was an intimation of the city's future. Mussolini built the road bridge to the mainland.

Stucky mill will have its time again, as a hotel

Venice Today

After WWII, industrial expansion on the mainland continued with the creation of a petrochemical complex that was good for the economy but noxious to the lagoon. In 1966 record floods devastated the city and it became apparent that it might one day be engulfed. People began to vote with their feet – the population today is less than half of what it was in the 1950s. Tourism, the annual film festival on the Lido, and the arts and architecture Biennales keep Venice in the spotlight, but its long-term future as a functioning city seems uncertain.

ENVIRONMENT

Formed 6000 years ago by the meeting of the sea with freshwater streams running off Alpine rivers, the lagoon is like a shallow dish, crisscrossed by navigable channels (some natural, others of human construction). More than 40 islands dot the lagoon, the seaward side of which is protected by a 50km arc of long, narrow islands (including the Lido) that staunch the inward flow of the Adriatic.

From the 16th century, lagoon maintenance was stepped up with the diversion of freshwater streams away from the area around Venice. The 20th century brought more drastic changes. In the 1960s a deep channel was dug through to the petrochemical complex in Porto Marghera, which lets in supertankers and too much seawater.

> **BRAGADIN BITES THE DUST**
> When the Turks took Famagusta (Cyprus) in 1570, they reserved a special fate for its Venetian commander, Marcantonio Bragadin. Having lopped off his nose and ears and left him to rot in jail for a couple of weeks, his captors publicly skinned him alive. One account says he only passed out when they reached his waist. The corpse was beheaded and the skin stuffed and sent to Constantinople. His remains, stolen in 1596, lie in the SS Giovanni e Paolo church (p32).

Get thee to the Campanile! *Acqua alta* (high water) is considered to be 0.8m above average sea level

SIREN CALL

Acqua alta (high water) officially begins at 0.8m above average sea level. Sixteen air-raid sirens around the city go off if it is expected to hit 1.1m. Over 1.2m you can be in trouble, as even the walkways set up in strategic parts of town are no use, and at 1.4m a state of emergency is declared. The November 1966 flood level was 1.94m.

Flooding in Venice has always been a problem. In winter high Adriatic tides push into the lagoon and inundate the city. Record floods in 1966 set alarm bells ringing and in 2003 work began on the controversial Mose project to fit the lagoon's sea entrances with mobile barriers. If all goes well, they could be in place by 2012, although it remains unclear if they will work. The combination of subsidence (at least 14cm in the 20th century) and rising average sea levels (9cm) means the city is literally sinking!

GOVERNMENT & POLITICS

Venice is the capital of the Veneto region (one of 20 regions in Italy), which extends west to Verona and Lake Garda and north into the Alps. The region is subdivided into seven provinces, of which the area around Venice – Venezia – is one.

Since 1927 the *comune* (municipality) of Venice has comprised the islands of the lagoon (including Murano, Burano, Torcello, the Lido and Pellestrina), as well as Mestre, Porto Marghera and Chioggia and other centres on the mainland. Locals divide the lot into three areas: *terraferma* (mainland), *centro storico* (Venice proper, including Giudecca) and *estuario* (remaining islands). Venice is made up of six *sestieri* (neighbourhoods).

In 2005 centre-left philosopher Massimo Cacciari became mayor of Venice again after some time in the political wilderness. An opponent of the Mose barriers project, he is looking into putting a stop to the already advanced work on the project. Another hot potato he inherited is the interminable saga of the Grand Canal's fourth bridge, designed by and named after world-renowned architect Santiago Calatrava. It is just possible it will be in place by the time you read this, but no-one in Venice is holding their breath!

Bird's-eye view of Piazza San Marco (p29) from the basilica: the pigeons get it for free

ECONOMY

The mainstays of Venice's economy are tourism and the mainland petro-chemical industry in Porto Marghera. The Veneto region, long a rural backwater, took off in the 1970s and '80s due to small industries and family businesses (such as the Treviso-based Benetton). The Veneto contains almost 8% of Italy's population and contributes about 15% of exports.

Tourism is pivotal in Venice. In 2005 some 3.3 million visitors stayed at least one night in the lagoon city. Up to 25 million day-trippers pour in annually.

> **DID YOU KNOW?**
> • Population 63,500 (Venice proper), 271,000 (total municipality)
> • The city is carved up by 150 canals
> • The city's canals are crossed by 416 bridges
> • In 2005 19% of foreign visitors to the Veneto region were German

Of the lagoon's remaining traditional industries (including boat-building and fishing), glass-making has the highest profile. Although much is clearly directed at the tourist trade, some of the work coming out of Murano's glass factories is of the highest quality.

SOCIETY & CULTURE

With so many tourists wandering around, finding a full-blooded Venetian can be a tall order! Some of the great aristocratic names survive and their families often retain enormous lodgings in the city's grander palaces. Small pockets of working-class Venetians and fishing families also continue to live in the city, shoulder to shoulder with a student population made up of locals and people from all over the country.

Venice's population is 63,500 (that's people, not pigeons, if you were tempted to ask)

An island city, Venice has something of a village feel – there is no car culture and people are obliged to walk around or use public transport. Locals frequently run into friends or acquaintances, stop for a chat or a quick *ombra* (glass of wine) and then head on their way. Venetians manage the neat conjuring trick of somehow not really *seeing* the floods of visitors around them.

Venetians love a sociable tipple in the city's bars and squares. In summer, some zip off on speedboats to lagoon beaches on Sant'Erasmo or catch the ferry to the Lido for the seaside. The winter chic crowds head off to ski in Cortina in the Alps.

Fondaco dei Turchi (p24) – beware the resident Ouransaurus!

ARTS
Architecture

Apart from a few Roman vestiges on Torcello and the mainland, the earliest reminders we have of building in the lagoon are the 7th- and 9th-century apses of the Cattedrale di Santa Maria Assunta on Torcello (p19). The church is a mix of Byzantine and Romanesque. The latter style developed in the West and is characterised by the use of the semicircle. Byzantine influences are clearest in the use of decorative mosaics.

The grandest example of style-mixing is the Basilica di San Marco (p9). Redolent of Istanbul, it is a grand Byzantine work, with touches ranging from Romanesque to Renaissance.

Venice put its own spin on Gothic. The two grand churches of the Franciscan and Dominican orders – the Santa Maria Gloriosa dei Frari (p14) and SS Giovanni e Paolo (p32) – are towering, austere creations built in brick and eschewing external decoration. The white-and-pink marble Palazzo Ducale (p10) is the most stunning example of late Gothic secular construction.

The Renaissance brought a return to the study of classical lines, clear in Andrea Palladio's (1508–80) San Giorgio Maggiore (p22) and SS Redentore (p33) churches. Jacopo Sansovino (1486–1570) was another key Renaissance architect. The baroque architect Baldassare Longhena (1598–1682) dominated the 17th century, just as his Santa Maria della Salute (p23) presides over the south end of the Grand Canal.

Painting

The glory days of Venetian art came with the Renaissance, starting with the Bellini family, especially Giovanni. He was followed by Vittore Carpaccio (1460–1526), Cima da Conegliano (c1459–c1517), Giorgione

(1477–1510) and Lorenzo Lotto (c1480–1556). They laid the foundations for what was to come, a starburst of greatness that thrust Venice into the forefront of European painting.

When his *Assunta* (Assumption) was unveiled in the Santa Maria Gloriosa dei Frari church (p14), Titian (c1490–1576) was revealed as an unparalleled genius of the late Renaissance. He only just overshadowed Tintoretto (1518–94), best known for his paintings that fill the Scuola Grande di San Rocco (p15), and Paolo Veronese (1528–88), who had a hand in the decoration of the Palazzo Ducale (p10).

Giambattista Tiepolo (1696–1770) was the uncontested king of Venetian rococo, followed by his son Giandomenico (1727–1804). At about the same time, the *vedutisti* (landscape painters) were also at work. The photo-sharp images of Venice by Canaletto (1697–1768) are known the world over.

Sculpture

Fine Romanesque sculpture adorns the Basilica di San Marco, and some of the *doges'* tombs in the church of SS Giovanni e Paolo are worthy Gothic-era contributions.

Antonio Canova (1757–1822), born in Possagno, spent his early years in Venice but ended up in Rome as the country's most celebrated sculptor. A sprinkling of his works can be seen in the Museo Correr (p24).

Music

Venice's greatest musical son was Antonio Vivaldi (1678–1741), a Castello lad. He left a vast repertoire behind, of which the best concerto is *Le Quattro Stagioni* (The Four Seasons). You can visit his church, La Pietà, on Riva degli Shiavoni, Castello. Tomaso Albinoni (1671–1750) also produced some exquisite music, including the sublime *Adagio in G Minor*.

Relics from the 7th to 13th centuries flank the entrance to the Museo di Torcello (p19)

ARRIVAL & DEPARTURE
Air
Most flights arrive at Marco Polo Airport (1, D2), 12km from the city, on the mainland. Others arrive at Treviso's San Giuseppe Airport (1, D1), 30km north of Venice.

MARCO POLO AIRPORT
Information

General Enquiries & Flight Information ☎ 041 260 92 60

Airport Access
Bus services run to Piazzale Roma (2, C4) via Mestre station (5, B1).

ATVO Fly Bus (☎ 0421 38 36 72; www .atvo.it; €3)

Azienda Consorzio Trasporti Veneziano (ACTV; ☎ 041 24 24; €1) City bus No 5 also serves the airport.

The fast ferry from the airport costs €11 to Venice (1¼ hours) or the Lido (one hour) and €6 to Murano (30 minutes). Pick it up at the Zattere (2, D5) or in front of the Giardini ex Reali (3, H5). A faster, direct service (the gold line) from San Marco (stopping only at nearby San Zaccaria; 2, F5) costs €25 and runs eight times a day.

Alilaguna (☎ 041 523 57 75; www .alilaguna.it)

You will probably pay up to €90 for the 30-minute water taxi ride between the airport and Piazzetta San Marco (3, H5), for up to four people including luggage.

Reckon on €35 from the airport to Piazzale Roma (2, C4; 15 minutes) for a land taxi.

SAN GIUSEPPE AIRPORT
Information

General Enquiries & Flight Information ☎ 0422 31 51 11

Airport Access
The **Eurobus** (☎ 0421 38 36 71) service runs to/from Piazzale Roma (2, C4; one way/return €5/9).

Local bus No 6 goes to the main train station in Treviso. From there you can proceed to Venice by rail.

Bus
The main trans-European bus company, **Eurolines** (www.eurolines.com), is represented by **Agenzia Brusutti** (2, B4; ☎ 041 520 55 30; Piazzale Roma 497/e).

Train
Trenitalia (☎ 89 20 21; www.trenitalia .it) operates services from most major Italian cities. Direct international trains run to Venice from Geneva, Munich and Vienna. All stop at Stazione di Santa Lucia (2, C3) and Mestre (5, B1), on the mainland.

Boat
Ferries run year round from Greece to Venice. Contact **Minoan Lines** (www .minoan.gr), which is at the passenger port (Stazione Marittima; 2, B3). Summer boats, **Venezia Lines** (www.venezialines .com), run to Croatia from the old Stazione Marittima (3, A6).

Travel Documents
PASSPORT
You need a valid passport (or ID card for EU, Norwegian and Swiss citizens) to enter Italy.

VISA
Nationals of Australia, Canada, Israel, Japan, New Zealand and the USA don't need a visa if entering as tourists for up to 90 days. Others and those wishing to stay longer should check with Italian consulates.

Customs & Duty Free
People entering Italy from outside the EU may bring in duty free up to one bottle of spirits, one bottle of wine, 50mL of perfume and 200 cigarettes. People travelling within the EU are allowed to import VAT-free goods (on sale at European airports).

Left Luggage
The *deposito* (left luggage) at Marco Polo Airport is in the arrivals hall. There is no such facility at San Giuseppe Airport.

GETTING AROUND

Walking is best but there are other options. The **ACTV** (www.actv.it) runs the *vaporetto* (water bus) network in Venice and buses to Mestre and other mainland areas. Water taxis are snazzy but pricey.

Travel Passes

Best value for *vaporetti* is a *biglietto a tempo*, a ticket that is valid on all transport (except the Alilaguna, Clodia, Fusina and LineaBlù services) for 24 hours from the first validation (€12). *Biglietto tre giorni,* a three-day version, costs €25 (€15 with a Rolling Venice pass; see Student & Youth Cards, opposite). Buy passes at ACTV and Vela outlets.

The **Venice Card** (☎ 041 24 24; www .venicecard.it) is another option but it doesn't represent any saving. The blue card gives unlimited use of transport for one, three or seven days, free access to public toilets (otherwise €0.50) and some discounts in shops, bars, restaurants and car parks. The orange version throws in a series of sights.

The junior (under 30) cards cost €15/30/47 for one/three/seven days, while the senior versions cost €17/34/52. The junior orange cards cost €22/45/67 and the senior versions €29/54/76.

Vaporetto

Several *vaporetto* lines run up and down the Grand Canal, although some are *limitato* (limited stops) services. Line No 1 is an all-stops job that takes a little over 30 minutes between Ferrovia (3, A1) and San Marco (3, H5).

Tickets must be bought in advance and validated prior to boarding. Single-trip tickets cost €5, so travel passes make good sense. Timetables are posted at stops. Some lines start as early as 5.30am and others stop as early as 9pm. A night (N) service runs along the Grand Canal and serves the Lido (5, E3) and Giudecca (2, C6). Similar services also serve the main lagoon islands. None operates past about 4.30am.

Traghetto

The *traghetto* is a commuter gondola that crosses the Grand Canal at strategic spots and saves on shoe leather. Some operate from about 9am to 6pm, while others stop at around noon. A crossing costs €0.50 and passengers stand.

Water Taxi

Water taxis (☎ 041 522 23 03, 041 240 67 11) are expensive, with a flagfall of €8.70 and €1.30 for every minute of travel, an extra €6 if you order one by telephone, and various surcharges. A typical trip across Venice will cost around €50 for up to four passengers. Rogue water taxi operators work the Tronchetto area and Piazzale Roma, insisting there are no *vaporetti* nearby. Ignore them and head for the *vaporetto* stops.

Bus

Regular buses (including a night service) run from Piazzale Roma (2, C4) to Mestre and other mainland destinations. Tickets to Mestre cost €1 (or €9 for 10 rides) and must be bought at newsstands or tobacconists prior to boarding.

Train

All trains leaving Stazione di Santa Lucia (2, C3) stop in Mestre. Tickets (available from newsstands at the train station) cost €1 on the regular, slower trains. The last trains run around midnight – check timetables posted at either train station.

Taxi

You can call a **taxi** (☎ 041 93 62 22) for trips to Mestre or the airport starting from Piazzale Roma (2, C4), or just turn up at the taxi ranks.

Car & Motorcycle

You cannot drive anywhere in Venice, except off to the mainland from the car parks around Piazzale Roma (2, C4) and Tronchetto (2, A3).

PRACTICALITIES

Business Hours
Public offices open from around 8.30am to 2pm Monday to Friday. Regular business hours are around 8.30am to 1.30pm and 4pm to 7.30pm Monday to Friday. A few larger stores open through lunch. Many open on Saturday and some even on Sunday. Many shops close on Monday morning.

Banks generally open from 8.30am to 1.30pm and 3.30pm to 4.30pm. Some main branches also open from 9am to 12.30pm on Saturday. Hours vary from bank to bank. Bureaux de change tend to open from 8am to 8pm Monday to Saturday.

Climate & When to Go
The city is busiest in spring (Easter to June) and early autumn (September to October). Accommodation can also be hard to find around Christmas, New Year and Carnevale (February). July and August tend to be oppressively hot and humid, while winter can be grey and wet, with frequent flooding in November and December. Venice is at its best in early spring, although late winter, when the skies are often crisp and blue and the crowds much reduced, is tempting.

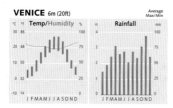

Disabled Travellers
The map from Azienda di Promozione Turistica (APT) offices (see Tourist Information, p88) has areas of the city shaded in yellow, indicating they can be negotiated without running into a bridge. Some bridges are equipped with *servoscale* (lifts), marked on the maps. You can (in theory) get hold of a key to these lifts from tourist offices. *Vaporetto* lines 1 and 82 and the bigger lagoon ferries have access for wheelchairs. Passengers in wheelchairs travel for free. Six bus lines are adapted for wheelchair users, including No 2 (Piazzale Roma to Mestre train station) and those for the airport.

Modifications have been made to some of the city's sights to facilitate access for those in wheelchairs.

INFORMATION & ORGANISATIONS
A **disabled assistance office** (☯ 7am-9pm daily) is located in front of platform 4 at Venice's Santa Lucia station (3, A1).

You could also try **Informahandicap** (3, F3; ☎ 041 274 81 44; www.comune .venezia.it/informahandicap (in Italian); Ca' Farsetti, San Marco 4136; ☯ 3-5pm Wed). The website has information on hotels that can accommodate disabled guests, getting around the city and other information.

Accessible Travel & Leisure (☎ 01452-729739; www.accessibletravel.co.uk; Avionics House, Naas Lane, Gloucester GL2 2SN) claims to be the biggest UK travel agent dealing with travel for the disabled.

Allegro in Venice (p43) offers aid and tours to disabled visitors to the city.

Discounts
Admission to state museums (there are just three in Venice) is free for EU citizens under 18 and over 65. Otherwise there are precious few reductions for sights and none (except for students resident in Venice) for public transport.

STUDENT & YOUTH CARDS
International student cards don't open many doors in Venice. Those aged 14 to 29 can obtain a Rolling Venice card (€3) at tourist offices and Vela outlets (3, B1).

Electricity
Voltage	220V
Frequency	50Hz
Cycle	AC
Plugs	standard continental (two round pins)

Embassies & Consulates

Most countries have embassies in Rome. A few have consulates in Venice. Where there is no representation in Venice, the nearest available embassy or consulate is listed:

Australia (☎ 02 7770 4227; Via Borgogna 2, Milan)

Canada (☎ 049 876 48 33; Riviera Ruzzante 25, Padua)

New Zealand (☎ 06 441 71 71; Via Zara 28, Rome)

UK (5, B1; ☎ 041 505 59 90; Piazzale Donatori di Sangue 2, Mestre)

USA (☎ 02 29 03 51; Via Principe Amedeo 2/10, Milan)

Emergencies

Ambulance	☎ 118
Carabinieri (military police)	☎ 112
Fire	☎ 115
Police	☎ 113

Fitness

A couple of small municipal swimming pools operate (except in summer), with complex timetables (contact them for details), along with a handful of small gyms.

GYMS

Palestra Oasi (3, B5; ☎ 041 296 05 05; Fondamenta dello Squero, Dorsoduro 3076; ⏲ 9am-10pm Mon-Fri, 9am-12.30pm Sat; 🚤 San Basilio) Sign-up fee €25 and block of 10 entries (valid for 10 weeks) €70.

SWIMMING POOLS

Piscina Comunale A Chimisso (2, B6; ☎ 041 528 54 30; Sacca S Biagio, Giudecca; admission €5, 10 tickets €43; ⏲ Sep-Jun; 🚤 Sacca Fisola)

Gay & Lesbian Travellers

Homosexuality is legal in Italy and well tolerated in Venice and the north in general. The legal age of consent is 16. In Venice there's little in the way of a gay scene, with no overtly gay establishments.

Health
PRECAUTIONS

Venice's tap water is safe to drink (although many people prefer the bottled stuff) and food preparation is generally hygienic. Heat and humidity might be a problem in the summer – wear a hat and loose, comfortable clothing and drink plenty of fluids.

MEDICAL SERVICES

Hospitals with 24-hour emergency departments include the following:

Ospedale Civile (3, J2; ☎ 041 529 41 11; Campo SS Giovanni e Paolo, Castello 5666)

Ospedale Umberto I (5, B1; ☎ 800 501 060 toll free; Via Circonvallazione 50, Mestre)

DENTAL SERVICES

Urgent dental treatment is available at Ospedale Civile (see Medical Services, above).

PHARMACIES

Farmacie (pharmacies) usually open from 9am to 12.30pm and 3.30pm to 7.30pm. Most close on Saturday afternoon and Sunday. Information on all-night pharmacies is listed in *Un Ospite di Venezia,* a free booklet available at tourist offices and some hotels.

Holidays

1 January	New Year's Day
6 January	Epiphany
March/April	Good Friday
March/April	Easter Monday
25 April	Liberation Day
1 May	Labour Day
15 August	Feast of the Assumption
1 November	All Saints' Day
8 December	Feast of the Immaculate Conception
25 December	Christmas Day
26 December	Boxing Day

Internet
INTERNET CAFÉS

Planet Internet (4, B2; ☎ 041 524 41 88; Rio Terà San Leonardo, Cannaregio 1519; per hr €8 ⏲ 9am-11pm)

World House (3, J4; ☎ 041 528 48 71; www.world-house.org; Calle della Chiesa, Castello 4502; 31-60 min €8, 3hr €18 ☽ 10am-11pm)

USEFUL WEBSITES

LonelyPlanet.com (www.lonelyplanet .com) has links to many Venetian websites. Others include the following:

Comune di Venezia (www.comune .venezia.it)

Ombra.Net (www.ombra.net)

Venice Blog (http://veniceblog .typepad.com)

Lost Property

For items lost on *vaporetti* call ☎ 041 272 21 79, or on trains call ☎ 041 78 55 31. Otherwise call the *vigili urbani* (local police) on ☎ 041 522 45 76. The lost property office is at Piazzale Roma (3, A2).

Metric System

Metric is standard and Italians use commas in decimals and points to indicate thousands.

TEMPERATURE
°C = (°F - 32) ÷ 1.8
°F = (°C x 1.8) + 32

DISTANCE
1in = 2.54cm
1cm = 0.39in
1m = 3.3ft = 1.1yd
1ft = 0.3m
1km = 0.62 miles
1 mile = 1.6km

WEIGHT
1kg = 2.2lb
1lb = 0.45kg
1g = 0.04oz
1oz = 28g

VOLUME
1L = 0.26 US gallons
1 US gallon = 3.8L
1L = 0.22 imperial gallons
1 imperial gallon = 4.55L

Money
ATMS

Automatic Teller Machines (ATMs) are concentrated in busy areas along Lista di Spagna (4, B3) and Strada Nova (3, F1) and around the train station (3, A1); also try around the Rialto (3, G2) and Piazza San Marco (3, H5).

CREDIT CARDS

Visa and MasterCard are the most widely accepted cards. Small hotels and restaurants sometimes don't take cards. For 24-hour card cancellations or assistance, call:

Amex	☎ 800 864 046
Diners Club	☎ 06 357 53 33
MasterCard	☎ 800 870 866
Visa	☎ 800 819 014

CURRENCY

Italy's currency is the euro. There are seven euro notes in denominations of €500, €200, €100, €50, €20, €10 and €5. The eight euro coins come in denominations of €2 and €1, then 50, 20, 10, five, two and one cents.

MONEYCHANGERS

Banks and the post office generally offer the fairest rates and lowest commissions. The latter can vary from a fixed fee of €1.50 to a percentage. Bureaux de change commissions can be hefty (as high as 10%!).

TRAVELLERS CHEQUES

Travellers cheques can be cashed at any bank or exchange office (watch commissions). **American Express** (3, G5; ☎ 041 520 08 44; Salizada San Moisè, San Marco 1471; ☽ 9am-5.30pm Mon-Fri, 9am-12.30pm Sat) **Travelex** (3, H4; ☎ 041 528 73 58; Piazza San Marco 142; ☽ 9am-6pm Mon-Sat, 9.30am-5pm Sun) Has a branch at Riva del Ferro 5126 (3, G3).

Newspapers & Magazines

The major Italian dailies include *Corriere della Sera* and *La Repubblica*. The local dailies are *Il Gazzettino* and *Nuova Venezia*. A handy local publication is *VeNews*, a monthly magazine with listings in Italian and English. Ask also for *La Rivista di Venezia*, which is published by the tourist board.

Post

The main **post office** (3, G3; ☎ 160; www
.poste.it; Salizada del Fondaco dei Tedeschi;
🕑 8.30am-6.30pm Mon-Fri, 8.30am-1pm
Sat) is near the Ponte di Rialto. You can buy
stamps here or from tobacconists (look for
the *tabacchi* sign).

POSTAL RATES

Postcards and letters up to 20g sent *posta
prioritaria* (priority post) cost €1 to Australia
and New Zealand, €0.85 to the Americas,
€0.65 within Europe and to Mediterranean
countries, and €0.60 within Italy.

Radio

There are three state-owned stations: RAI-1
(1332AM or 89.7FM), RAI-2 (846AM or
91.7FM) and RAI-3 (93.7FM). Radio Venezia
(101.1FM) has news and a reasonable selection of music.

Telephone

A local call on a public phone costs €0.25 to
€0.30 for three minutes. Orange Telecom Italia
phone booths are spread across the city.

PHONECARDS

Telecom Italia phonecards (€2.50 or €5) are
available from post offices, tobacconists and
some newsstands. Some internet centres
provide cut-rate international call facilities.

MOBILE PHONES

Italy uses the GSM cellular phone system,
compatible with phones sold in the rest of
Europe, Australia and most of Asia, but not
those from North America and Japan (unless you have a tri-band handset).

COUNTRY & CITY CODES

The city code (including the 0) is an integral
part of the number and must be dialled,
whether calling from next door or abroad;
mobile numbers have no initial 0. The country and city codes are:

Italy	☎ 39
Venice	☎ 041

USEFUL PHONE NUMBERS

Local Directory Enquiries	☎ 12
International Directory Enquiries	☎ 176
International Operator	☎ 170
International Access Code	☎ 00

Television

The three state-run stations, RAI-1, RAI-2
and RAI-3, compete with the private Canale
5, Italia 1, Rete 4 and La 7 stations to provide a diet of talk shows and variety shows
and the occasional decent programme (especially on RAI-3). Many hotels have BBC
World, CNN, Sky Channel and others.

Time

Venice Standard Time is one hour ahead of
GMT/UTC. Daylight savings is practised from
the last Sunday in March to the last Sunday
in October.

Tipping

In restaurants where service is not included
it's customary to leave a 10% tip. In bars
Italians often leave small change. You
should tip the porter at upmarket hotels
(about €0.50 per bag).

Toilets

Public toilets are scattered about Venice –
look for the 'WC toilette' signs. Hours vary
but generally they open from 7am to 7pm.
Visitors pay €0.50, residents €0.25.

Tourist Information

In Venice there is one **central information
line** (☎ 041 529 87 11; www.turismoven
ezia.it).

The main APT office is at **Piazza San
Marco** (3, G5; Piazza San Marco 71/f;
🕑 9am-3.30pm Mon-Sat). Others are in the
Venice Pavilion (3, G5; 🕑 10am-6pm),
train station (3, B1; 🕑 8am-6.30pm),
Piazzale Roma (2, C4; Garage Comunale;
🕑 9.30am-1pm & 1.30-4.30pm) and the
arrivals hall of **Marco Polo Airport** (5, D1;
🕑 9.30am-7.30pm).

Women Travellers

Of the main destinations in Italy, Venice has to be the safest for women. If you do get unwanted attention, whatever methods you use to deal with it at home should work here.

Tampons (and more commonly sanitary towels) are available in pharmacies and supermarkets. Prescriptions are needed for the contraceptive pill.

LANGUAGE

True-blue Venetians speak a dialect (for some, a separate language) known commonly as Venessian. Here are some useful Italian phrases to get you started. Grab Lonely Planet's *Italian Phrasebook* to learn more.

Basics

Hello.	*Buongiorno.* (pol)
	Ciao. (inf)
Goodbye.	*Arrivederci.* (pol)
	Ciao. (inf)
Yes.	*Sì.*
No.	*No.*
Please.	*Per favore/*
	Per piacere.
Thank you (very much).	*(Mille) grazie.*
You're welcome.	*Prego.*
Excuse me.	*Mi scusi.*
Do you speak English?	*Parla inglese?*
I don't understand.	*Non capisco.*
Could you please write it down?	*Potrebbe scriverlo?*
How much is it?	*Quanto costa?*

Getting Around

When does the ... leave/arrive?	*A che ora parte/ arriva ...?*
bus	*l'autobus*
boat	*la barca*
train	*il treno*
a ... ticket	*un biglietto di ...*
one-way	*solo andata*
return	*andata e ritorno*
Where is ...?	*Dov'è ...?*

Accommodation

Do you have any rooms available?	*Avete delle camere libere?*
a ... room	*una camera ...*
single	*singola*
twin	*doppia*
double	*matrimoniale*

Around Town

I'm looking for ...	*Cerco ...*
the market	*il mercato*
a public toilet	*un gabinetto*
What time does it open/close?	*A che ora (si) apre/ chiude?*

Eating

breakfast	*prima colazione*
lunch	*pranzo*
dinner	*cena*
snack	*spuntino/merenda*
The bill, please.	*Il conto, per favore.*
Is service included in the bill?	*Il servizio è compreso nel conto?*
Can you recommend a ...?	*Potrebbe consigliare un ...?*
bar/pub	*bar/pub*
café	*bar*
restaurant	*ristorante*

Entertainment

What's on ...?	*Che c'è in programma ...?*
locally	*in zona*
this weekend	*questo fine settimana*
today	*oggi*
tonight	*stasera*
Is there a local entertainment guide?	*C'è una guida agli spettacoli in città?*

Time, Days & Numbers

What time is it?	*Che ora è?*
Monday	*lunedì*
Tuesday	*martedì*
Wednesday	*mercoledì*
Thursday	*giovedì*
Friday	*venerdì*

Saturday	*sabato*
Sunday	*domenica*

1	*uno*
2	*due*
3	*tre*
4	*quattro*
5	*cinque*
6	*sei*
7	*sette*
8	*otto*
9	*nove*
10	*dieci*
50	*cinquanta*
100	*cento*
1000	*mille*
2000	*duemila*

Banking

I'd like to ...	*Vorrei ...*
cash a cheque	*riscuotere un assegno*
change money	*cambiare denaro*
change some travellers cheques	*cambiare degli assegni di viaggio*

Where's the nearest ...?	*Dov'è il ... più vicino?*
ATM	*bancomat*
foreign exchange office	*cambio*

Post

Where's the post office?	*Dov'è la posta?*

I want to send a ...	*Voglio spedire ...*
parcel	*un pachetto*
postcard	*una cartolina*

I want to buy ...	*Voglio comprare ...*
an envelope	*una busta*
a postage stamp	*un francobollo*

Phone & Mobile Phones

I want to buy a phone card.	*Voglio comprare una scheda telefonica.*

I want to make ... a call (to ...)	*Voglio fare ... una chiamata (a ...)*
reverse-charge/ collect call	*una chiamata a carico del destinatario*

Where can I find a/an ...?	*Dove si trova un ...?*
I'd like a/an ...	*Vorrei un...*
adaptor plug	*addattatore*
charger for my phone	*caricabatterie*
mobile/cell phone for hire	*cellulare da noleggiare*
prepaid mobile/ cell phone	*cellulare prepagato*
SIM card for your network	*SIM card per vostra rete telefonica*

Internet

Where's the local internet café?	*Dove si trova l'internet point?*

I'd like to ...	*Vorrei ...*
check my email	*controllare le mie email*
get online	*collegarmi a internet*

Emergencies

It's an emergency!	*È un'emergenza!*
Could you please help me/us?	*Mi/Ci può aiutare, per favore?*

Call ...!	*Chiami ...!*
the police	*la polizia*
a doctor	*un medico*
an ambulance	*un'ambulanza*

Where's the police station?	*Dov'è la questura?*

Health

Where's the nearest ...?	*Dov'è ... più vicino?*
chemist	*la farmacia*
(night)	*(di turno)*
dentist	*il dentista*
doctor	*il medico*
hospital	*l'ospedale*

I need a doctor (who speaks English).	*Ho bisogno di un medico (che parli inglese).*

Index

See also separate subindexes for Eating (p94), Entertainment (p94), Shopping (p94), Sights with map references (p94-5) and Sleeping (p95).

SLEEPING

FEATURES

Ristorante Riviera	*Eating*
Teatro La Fenice	*Entertainment*
Aurora	*Drinking*
Palazzo Ducale	*Highlights*
Vivaldi Store	*Shopping*
Museo Storico Navale	*Sights/Activities*
Hotel Flora	*Sleeping*

AREAS

	Beach, Desert
	Building
	Land
	Mall
	Other Area
	Park/Cemetary
	Sports
	Urban

HYDROGRAPHY

	River, Creek
	Intermittent River
	Canal
	Swamp
	Water

BOUNDARIES

	State, Provincial
	International
	Ancient Wall

ROUTES

	Tollway
	Freeway
	Primary Road
	Secondary Road
	Tertiary Road
	Lane
	Under Construction
	One-Way Street
	Unsealed Road
	Mall/Steps
	Tunnel
	Walking Path
	Walking Trail
	Track
	Walking Tour

TRANSPORT

	Airport, Airfield
	Bus Route
	Cycling, Bicycle Path
	Ferry
	General Transport
	Metro
	Monorail
	Rail
	Taxi Rank
	Tram

SYMBOLS

	Bank, ATM
	Buddhist
	Castle, Fortress
	Christian
	Diving, Snorkeling
	Embassy, Consulate
	Hospital, Clinic
	Information
	Internet Access
	Islamic
	Jewish
	Lookout
	Monument
	Mountain
	National Park
	Parking Area
	Petrol Station
	Picnic Area
	Point of Interest
	Police Station
	Post Office
	Ruin
	Swimming Pool
	Telephone
	Toilets
	Waterfall
	Zoo, Bird Sanctuary